BEYOND HIDDEN NARCISSIST

Protect Yourself from Emotional Abuse in a Narcissistic Relationship and Discover How Parents and Partners with Narcissistic Personality Disorders Manipulate Their Victims

Melanie White

COPYRIGHT © 2020 BY Melanie White

All rights reserved. No part of this publication may be reproduced, distributed, or transmitted in any form or by any means, including photocopying, recording, or other electronic or mechanical methods, without the prior written permission of the publisher, except in the case of brief quotations embodied in critical reviews and certain other noncommercial uses permitted by copyright law.

TABLE OF CONTENTS

INTRODUCTION	7

CHAPTER 1 — 9

WHO IS A NARCISSIST	9
Types of Narcissistic	14

CHAPTER 2 — 19

CHARACTERISTICS OF THE NARCISSISTIC PERSON	19
Narcissism characteristics in women	31
Narcissism Characteristics in Men	37
Differences between Narcissism and Self-Esteem	38

CHAPTER 3 — 43

THESE ARE THE TRAITS THAT DEFINE THEM	43
Strategies to Protect Yourself from a Narcissistic Person	48
Signs That You Are Raising a Narcissistic Child	52

CHAPTER 4 — 57

THE LOVE BETWEEN AN EMPATH AND A NARCISSIST	57

CHAPTER 5 — 63

SIGNS OF GASLIGHTING IN A NARCISSISTIC RELATIONSHIP — 63

CHAPTER 6 — 71

NARCISSISM IN RELATIONSHIP — 71
- Signs That Your Partner Is Narcissistic — 74
- How to act if you are dating a narcissist — 79
- Things You Can Expect in a Relationship with a Narcissist — 80

CHAPTER 7 — 87

HOW NARCISSISTS MANIPULATE THEIR VICTIMS — 87
- Things You Shouldn't Do In Dealing with Narcissists — 92

CHAPTER 8 — 94

THE DIFFERENCE BETWEEN SELF-ESTEEM AND NARCISSISM — 94
- Tricks That Narcissus Uses To Lower Your Self-Esteem — 97

CHAPTER 9 — 102

NARCISSIST ABUSE CYCLE — 102
- The Narcissistic Abuse Cycle in Relationships — 103

CHAPTER 10 — 109
REASONS WHY NARCISSISTS CANNOT INTIMATE RELATIONSHIPS — 109

CHAPTER 11 — 115
PEOPLE WHO DON'T CARE ABOUT YOU — 115

CHAPTER 12 — 120
HOW TO DEFEND YOURSELF FROM PSYCHOLOGICAL ABUSE — 120

CHAPTER 13 — 124
HOW TO DEFEND YOURSELF FROM EMOTIONAL TAKERS — 124
How can I defend myself against emotional takers? — 127

CHAPTER 14 — 129
TOXIC AND UNPRODUCTIVE ENVIRONMENTS — 129

CHAPTER 15 — 135
MANIPULATE OTHERS — 135
Signs Of Psychological Manipulation Present In Each Technique. — 137

CHAPTER 16 — 141
DEAL WITH TOXIC PEOPLE — 141

CHAPTER 17 — 145
SEXUAL NARCISSISM — 145

CHAPTER 18 — 149
EMOTIONAL ABUSE IN RELATIONSHIPS — 149
How to recover from emotional abuse — 154

CHAPTER 19 — 160
HOW TO REBUILD MY SELF-ESTEEM AFTER THE RELATIONSHIP WITH A NARCISSIST — 160
CONCLUSION — 165

INTRODUCTION

Narcissism is a concept of psychoanalysis that defines the individual who overly admires his own image and has an excessive passion for himself.

The term is derived from the word "Narcissus," who, according to Greek mythology, was a beautiful young man who aroused the love of the nymph Echo. But Narcissus rejected that love and was therefore condemned to fall in love with his own image reflected in the water. Narcissus eventually committed suicide by drowning. Later, Mother Earth turned him into a flower (daffodil).

Being related to auto-eroticism, narcissism consists of a concentration of the sexual instinct over one's own body.

Narcissistic individuals are often closed, self-centered, and lonely.

According to psychoanalyst Sigmund Freud, narcissism is a normal feature in all human beings. It is related to the development of libido (sexual desire, eros).

In Freud's psychoanalytic line, narcissism as sexual perversion is a fixation of a transitional phase of childhood, in itself normal. It is correlated, in part, with homosexuality and exhibitionism, among other characteristics of sexual conduct.

Narcissism becomes a pathology, that is, it goes from the normal to the unhealthy state, when it conflicts with cultural and ethical ideas, becoming excessive and hindering the normal relations of the individual in the social environment.

According to Freud's studies, narcissism can be divided into two stages: primary narcissism (auto-erotic phase) and secondary narcissism (when the individual develops the ego and can differentiate itself - its desires and what attracts them - from the rest of the world).

CHAPTER 1

WHO IS A NARCISSIST

The Narcissistic people do not tend to frequent inquiries from professional psychology and mental health, but it is quite common that some patients refer to the problems following persons living with the narcissistic profile.

There are also people with Narcissistic Personality Disorder in many areas, and of course, even in public life or in the media.

What is narcissism?

We usually associate the Narcissistic Personality Disorder with personalities from the world of entertainment: artists, actors, singers, intellectuals ... They are those characters who, as they say colloquially, "fame has raised to their heads."

Of course, narcissism is not directly linked to a person's well-off socioeconomic position, but to the individual's self-perception (that is, the perception of their worth, regardless of their social or economic status). The true essence of Narcissistic Personality Disorder lies there: the narcissistic person is absolutely convinced that oneself is superior to other people. The narcissists compare systematically with the people around them, and consider no one above them, but do place many (or even all) below themselves.

In more technical terms, narcissism is characterized by a general pattern of grandeur, poor empathy in personal relationships, and the overwhelming need to be admired by others.

Who is a narcissistic person?

People who have Narcissistic Personality Disorder tend to show themselves as individuals with high self-esteem. This high self-confidence does not make them better people since in the field of interpersonal relationships, they have significant shortcomings.

The narcissist always needs to be considered on a higher level than other people, either because he does not support any trait of these relatives, or because he has become detached from his old contact with them. Because of this active disengagement from others, people with Narcissistic Personality Disorder lack an authentic interest in others, which we can summarize by their lack of empathy. They are not very worried about what might happen to people around them, but instead, focus all their attention on themselves.

They only approve third parties when they revolve around their orbit, when they positively reinforce them with flattery and thus ratify their self-perception and their airs of greatness. Unfortunately, it is common for some relatives and friends of narcissistic people to fulfill this role of unconditional "admirers," surprised by the halo of trust that the narcissist gives off.

The personality of the narcissists and their day-to-day

People who suffer some degree of Narcissistic Personality Disorder export their way of being self-sufficient and the air of grandeur beyond the family environment. Usually, they are the individuals who develop in life and take advantage of their way of thinking about themselves.

Narcissistic people often do not feel comfortable when they have to travel by public transport or when they have to enter a hospital, because they will tend to think they deserve better treatment or will complain if they are not granted certain privileges. In the case that they have a good job, they usually use their money to buy watches, shoes, clothes, or sports cars of high standing, because they consider that they are worthy of these badges. Their status and the image of success is significant for a narcissist.

The narcissist's speech tends to be self-referential. The narcissistic persons expect their words to receive superior attention; It is not uncommon for them to be petulantly talking about themselves, about their life, their (unquestionable) opinion about things, demanding full attention to everything they say.

Although we are used to seeing people of narcissistic profile on television or in the movies and can even consider them funny and eccentric, the truth is that routine personal dealing with a person with Narcissistic Personality Disorder can be irritating. In addition to their egocentric behavior that we have already commented on, they are also characterized as being very spiteful people and tend to maintain attitudes of resentment and revenge towards others. They usually enjoy making other people feel bad; in this way, they feed their ego and their feeling of superiority. They are competitive, and if they believe that someone can shade them, they will try to undermine the prestige and reputation of that person.

Diagnostic criteria of Narcissistic Personality Disorder

According to the classification prepared and published in the DSM-V-TR, Narcissistic Personality Disorder has the following signs that may be useful to mental health professionals when establishing a diagnosis:

- They feel an excessive sense of grandeur.
- They are permanently worried about fantasies of power, success, beauty, or love.
- They are people who think they are unique and who try to have their status recognized.
- They demand excessive admiration from others.
- They express their feeling of being in their right. That is, they have irrational expectations about the treatment they deserve.
- They take advantage of other people for their purposes (Machiavellianism).
- Lack of empathy, that is, they are unable to identify or recognize the feelings and emotions of other people.
- They feel envious of others or believe that others feel envy.
- They tend to be arrogant.

On the other hand, it should be remembered that people whose behaviors fall into the category of Narcissistic Personality Disorder can be very varied in their way of expressing this alteration. After all, each person is a world, and we cannot capture all the nuances of someone's personality based on diagnostic manuals.

Types of Narcissistic

Having good self-esteem is essential in many aspects of our lives. This factor makes it easier for us to get involved in essential projects capable of leading us to improve our quality of life; it makes things easier for us to socialize, and it helps that the crises and small defeats of day-to-day do not sink us completely.

However, like virtually any psychological factor linked to personality, an excess of self-esteem can bring problems ... both for oneself and for those around him. When these high levels of self-love become narcissistic, everything changes.

The different types of narcissism

We could define narcissism as a psychological predisposition to obtain the recognition of others in the form of expressly positive assessments or indirectly, with particularly respectful treatment mixed with admiration.

Besides, narcissistic people are characterized by complying with other traits that are consistent with that expansive self-love: ideas of grandiosity about oneself, the predisposition to underestimate the rest of people, and difficulties in empathizing, among other things.

It is a personality element that can be present in different degrees of intensity, so that the more extreme it is, the more likely it is to be framed in one of the groups of symptoms of a mental disorder. More so, not all people with a high level of narcissism have a mental disorder that significantly damages their quality of life.

But in the same way that we can find differences in the degrees of intensity of this mental phenomenon, it is also possible to recognize some qualitative differences in the ways in which narcissism is expressed. Specifically, Dr. Bruce Stevens offers a classification of types of narcissism that can help us better understand all the nuances of this element of personality.

1. Dependent

In this case, we are not talking about the stereotype of a person delighted to have known him, very happy with who he is and what he can get. Unlike, this type of narcissism is characterized by the despair with which others seek validation.

Thus, these people combine a certain feeling of very subtle superiority, on the one hand, with the realization that this superiority cannot be put into practice, and therefore it is necessary to receive special treatment to compensate for that situation.

Their desire to obtain approval from others gives them an obsessive character.

2. Powerful

It is a kind of narcissism focused on demonstrations of power, that is, imposing its will on the rest. Whoever presents it, enjoys subjugating those around him.

3. Fantasy

These types of narcissists isolate themselves in an imaginary world in which their feelings of greatness correspond to how they see themselves. The tendency to fantasize is, then, a way to resolve the incongruity of feeling unique while at the same time thinking they are mediocre in their concrete way of behaving on a daily basis.

4. Body-centered

This is one of the types of narcissism in which the image projected before others is given more importance. Specifically, all attention is focused on the assessment of the body itself, and on the way in which it corresponds to certain beauty canons.

Of course, this assessment of aesthetics also reflects the need to receive compliments and even on a regular basis.

5. Trickster

This category includes people who feel good about themselves when they think skilled in deceiving others in exchange for personal gain. It is a type of narcissism that has much in common with typically psychopathic traits.

6. Lover

It is a type of narcissism oriented to the life of a couple and love. In this case, the unreasonable expectations about the relationship with another person makes it very easy for them to enter into crisis.

The love bond is idealized, since it is held that one's self is a special love, and that is why, when problems arise, a constructive mentality is not adopted before them.

7. Salvador

The person sees himself as someone capable of transforming lives and, specifically, of educating other people to fit into a way of being that matches one's personality.

8. Furious

In this case, the person has a shallow frustration threshold when he detects that he has been disrespected or that he has not been treated with due diligence. As a result, unjustified outbursts of anger are frequent.

His social life is usually very rugged because any situation of ambiguity can lead to problems.

9. Martyr

In this form of narcissism, the ideas of grandiosity focus on the point that one is more worthy than usual because he suffers and because he sacrifices himself.

CHAPTER 2

CHARACTERISTICS OF THE NARCISSISTIC PERSON

All people have a unique way of being. Moreover, if we consult a psychiatry manual, we would see that we have some characteristics in common with certain personality disorders. So much so, that it is usual to make excessive use of the term *"narcissistic"* to describe difficult relatives, politicians, uncomfortable neighbors, and even Millennials. Now, is narcissism so widespread in the population? Are there as many narcissistic people as it seems?

In the first place, it is important to differentiate that small apex of *"narcissism"* that we could all have, and that would be associated instead with self- love, with that other more extreme behavior that demonstrates the development of a disorder. Let us, therefore, see what characteristics usually distinguish the actual narcissist.

We all meet a narcissist at some point in our lives. However, not all narcissistic people are clinical cases with difficulties in living with a high degree of well-being: some are only partially, in a way that is not always evident.

These are the persons who think they are better than anyone, who underestimate others and who, when challenged, tend to act aggressively because they feel that their ego is being threatened. Studies reveal that at least 6.2% of the population is narcissistic and that the majority are men. Narcissists are often associated with different problems, from behavioral disorders in childhood, addiction to physical exercise (for example, anorexia), depressive disorders, or anxiety.

Narcissists are empty people

The narcissists put on a mask because they are empty inside. What they appear to be is not really what is behind their facade. The narcissist makes friends easily since he is usually open, even sweet, to others at the beginning. But he has serious difficulties in maintaining relationships because it is difficult for someone else to really care. Narcissists' friends, sooner or later, tend to get away from these characters because of their selfishness and because they are not trustworthy.

Narcissists eventually give themselves away, for their need to always 'be first' does not help forge lasting friendships. And although they always show off their achievements, they are weak people in reality. They can be attractive and intelligent, and they can love being in public, but they become extremely cold people in private when nobody looks at them.

Now, that doesn't mean they don't surround themselves with people. Narcissistic people need others to feel that they are being admired. They fear loneliness, and they fear to be alone with themselves because this can mean doing a serious analysis of consciousness, which is the biggest nightmare for them. Narcissists fear to come into contact with their own reality for having to accept that their true "I" is not what they try to make others believe.

But how can we identify a narcissist? What clues do these people give us? We are going to discuss the key characteristics of a narcissistic person, so you can recognize that you are dealing with one of them.

1. Superficially charming

A narcissist seems very lovely at first sight. They are often smooth talkers, and they know how to wind everyone around in no time. The charm that you see is, unfortunately, not genuine.

The narcissist is going to charm people to control them.

They often have brilliant ideas and visions and only see other people as objects they use to achieve their goals.

Usually, you do not immediately notice that this behavior is not genuine.

Most people do not immediately realize that this is a narcissistic person. Often, the true nature of the narcissist only comes to the fore during a conflict.

In addition to the extroverted, charming narcissist, there is another kind of narcissist who is more introverted. The hidden narcissist is more challenging to recognize because he can keep his true nature hidden for longer.

This narcissist shows weak and pathetic behavior and tries to attract attention. Yet he doesn't want to be helped at all, as long as he gets that limitless attention.

2. Huge ego

Narcissists have a huge ego. They think they are better, smarter, more attractive, and more talented than anyone else.

They think that only they deserve the best, and if their environment does not agree with this, they can respond with indignation and even aggression.

Narcissists take everything for granted and only use others to get what they want.

Just think of speaking loudly, always knowing better, and showing arrogant behavior.

The ego always pops up. Narcissists want everyone to listen to them. Other people have to settle.

Hidden narcissists, however, are more subtle. Female narcissists, in particular, are going to play the victim to attract attention.

They are going to twist things or lie. Everyone is busy with them because they are so pathetic. However, they secretly enjoy this attention.

Pity is also attending, as long as they are the center of attention.

Other people usually do not realize this because narcissists can act so well.

3. Good actor

Narcissists put on a mask because they cannot show real emotions. They then act as if they are sympathetic, funny, and social.

They are excellent actors. However, the love and so-called warmth they display are feigned and full of ulterior motives.

Narcissists themselves still believe the hardest in their own drama. They have been faking all their lives and are no different. After a while, they are no longer even aware that they are playing a role.

Other people fall for it with open eyes because they have so much persuasion. Others also often cannot imagine that someone may have such a total lack of empathy.

In their immediate surroundings, the narcissists will often be able to get away for years with their excellent image until someone threatens to disturb their world.

If this happens, they will explode in anger with physical or verbal violence. However, they do not do this with witnesses, but in the sneak when no one else can see it.

4. You come in second place

If you are in a relationship with a narcissist, you always come in the second place.

Narcissists strive for a certain goal. This can be fame, money, power, and sex. Or all at once. Pursuing their goals is often at the expense of everything. You will, therefore, never come first for them.

Narcissists only think of themselves, so there is no room for someone else. A relationship does not have much value for an extreme narcissist.

5. Little empathy

Narcissists have little to no empathy, and that is a massive stumbling block for many people.

A narcissist cannot relate to other people's feelings. They have never learned to develop that characteristic. They are primarily obsessed with their own needs.

The needs of another leave them completely cold. He cannot understand or feel someone else's emotions, but he does expect that someone else does.

6. Sickly jealous

Narcissists are extremely possessive and jealous. They regard their partner as their property.

Yet narcissists themselves often cheat to treat their partner very paranoidly.

So he can easily accuse you of sharing the bed with someone else while he is doing it himself.

This extreme jealousy can translate into enormously controlling behavior. For example, he can keep a close eye on your phone to check you.

In a normal relationship, couples can simply talk about their problems with jealousy. This is impossible with a narcissistic partner.

The jealousy of narcissists is so extreme that it can lead to outbursts of anger and revenge.

7. Creates a victim role

A narcissist often places himself in the victim role.

They are so self-centered that they have a hard time committing to someone. They often use their past as an excuse for the problems they have.

They act as a victim to arouse sympathy from their partner. They come across as sensitive, tragic, and vulnerable, attracting people who would want to 'save' them.

They enjoy this to the fullest. However, the narcissist takes no responsibility whatsoever and passes everything on to other people.

8. Very sensitive to criticism

Narcissists think they are always right. Their opinion is the only one that counts. They usually do not even pay attention to someone else's opinion.

He will always make the mistake of the other person and will not tolerate it if you try to go against his opinion.

So if you criticize the narcissist, then this could cost you dearly. They can then really burst into anger.

What they say often means nothing. The fact that you are critical is reason enough for him to get angry. If he feels hurt, he will punish the other.

The narcissist always has his opinion about other people, but he cannot tolerate criticism himself.

9. No empathy

A narcissist is unable to show real emotions. Let alone that they can agree with someone else's feelings.

A lack of empathy is the most significant characteristic of the narcissist. Not everyone is very empathetic. The difference with a narcissist is that this is completely missing from him.

Narcissists cannot show empathy, so they have to fake this.

If you have been in a relationship with a narcissist for a while, you will notice that this feigned empathy will always feel nasty because, after a while, the narcissist will make less effort to fake empathy properly.

Narcissists have no real emotional connection with other people. They judge others according to the function they can have for their image. In a relationship, the narcissist can promise you anything.

It looks like a fairy tale. You think that you are finally loved and understood, but actually, there is nothing like that at all. They are always empty promises that are never fulfilled.

10. Pathological liar

Pathological lying means that the narcissist naturally lies.

For example, he can conceal the best fraud and adultery. The worst thing is that he doesn't feel guilty about his lies and deceit. He is lying in a very relaxed and convincing way. Narcissists are so good at this that they sometimes succeed in overcoming a lie detector.

The narcissist will also tell lies about you to others. His goal is to isolate you in order to gain even more power over you. Because a narcissist is so convincing, everyone will easily believe him.

11. Manipulative and make you feel guilty

Narcissists are very adept at manipulating other people. They know exactly what to do to get their way. They often dominate and humiliate other people.

They manipulate people emotionally. They do this so subtly that the other is often not even aware of it. Narcissists want the other person to feel dependent.

That way, they are vulnerable and easy to mold and manipulate.

The other person in the relationship often feels guilty and gets the feeling that the problem lies with him. Your confidence is crumbling more and more without you noticing.

As a partner of a narcissist, you always start doubting your own behavior. You begin to think that the problems lie with you and that you have to change something.

The narcissistic partner will always suggest this, and this will make you feel extremely insecure. You do not realize that he is manipulating you and making you feel guilty.

12. Want to have and keep power

Narcissists have an irresistible urge for power and will do everything to preserve that power. Even if this is at the expense of others.

Narcissists often focus on people who are weaker than them, for example, insecure people.

Someone with low self-confidence is the perfect prey for the narcissist.

He gets you completely in his power by pushing you into an increasingly weaker position.

Narcissists attach great importance to appearance, money, and a certain status. This offers safety, and in that way, it is considered essential.

He needs a lovely house, nice clothes, and expensive cars so that other people can admire him.

Many narcissists are only focused on gaining more and more money and power. The male narcissist often does not want his partner to go to work.

After all, he wants to have everything in his possession and often does not give the partner access to the finances. If a divorce follows later, this can be a significant disadvantage for the partner.

13. Immature behavior

Narcissists often exhibit very immature behavior. They think they can do whatever they want. Just like children, they do not always have the capacity to distinguish between good and evil.

Narcissists are not developed emotionally. This often has to do with unprocessed traumas from their past.

So they cannot behave emotionally in a relationship. And that just marks the absence of one of the essential pillars of a healthy relationship.

Narcissists cannot express their feelings; they have a fear of attachment and, just like children, cannot admit their mistakes. Narcissists will repeat their mistakes constantly because they don't learn from them.

14. Causing unnecessary drama

Narcissists often cause unnecessary tension.

If someone else is in the spotlight, for example, a family member having a birthday, the narcissist will somehow want to attract attention. He does this, for example, by making negative comments about the party.

Narcissists consciously want to spoil another's sense of happiness.

Because they can't stand another person feeling good and getting all the attention. They are very envious and not only with regard to material things, but they are also jealous of someone else's cheerful behavior.

The only option they have in this situation is to ruin that person's joy. In this way, they draw attention back to them, and they do not care whether this is positive or negative attention.

Narcissism Characteristics In Women

Statistically, 75% of narcissists are men, and in general, the differences between their behaviors are small. But in the manifestation of narcissism, there are some differences because they emphasize different things. For example, men usually emphasize intellect, power, aggression, money, or social status. Women tend to emphasize the body, looks, charm, sexuality, female, household "traits" or their children.

Narcissistic women assert themselves or with their body and may even manifest anorexia nervosa or bulimia. Or they flaunt and exploit their physical charms, their sexuality, and their social and cultural life by affirming their 'femininity.' They guarantee their source of worship through their more traditional gender roles, home to children, careers, suitable, their husbands, their feminine traits, and their role in society, etc.

Another difference is the way they react to treatment. Women are more likely to be involved in therapy because, as a rule, women are more likely to admit their psychological problems. Men are a little less inclined to publicize their problems (due to rooted machismo) - it does not necessarily mean that they are less likely to admit to themselves their emotional conflicts.

The general rule of the narcissistic person cannot be forgotten: the narcissist uses everything around him/her to obtain his/her source of narcissistic idolatry. As a rule in women, this source becomes a child because of the way our society is still structured and the fact that women are still the only ones giving birth. It is easier for women to think of their children as their extension because they were actually their physical extensions as they were connected in the womb, and thus there was a more intense and extensive interaction.

The narcissistic woman respects her children as significant sources for her ego, while the male narcissist is more likely to regard his children as a nuisance rather than as a source of gratification and supply. As we still live in a society of inequality, men have many narcissistic sources for their egos, while women struggle to maintain their most reliable source of supply, their children. So she starts early on an insidious indoctrination, guilt, emotional sanctions, deprivation, and other psychological mechanisms; she tries to induce a dependence on them that cannot be easily broken. There is no difference in behavioral psychodynamics between the male and female narcissists, but there is a difference in their narcissistic source choices.

The narcissistic woman exercises the same control technique as the narcissistic man, is emotionally abusive, masters of "control" through verbal force, keen thinking, and emotional blackmail. Such people cling to their belief system, no matter how many times they are confronted with contrary evidence, however wrong they may be, the more drama and indignation they may exhibit.

Here are some common control tactics of a narcissistic woman:

- The narcissistic woman begins a conversation or attack with a topic. When you start presenting facts that are contrary to her beliefs, however sincere they may be to you, you are never right. She goes off tangent, changes the subject, or makes a new accusation. While you are still defending your original point of view, she has already taken from her hat another series of problems, blame, and topics that may even be completely unrelated.
- She says, shut up! In explaining your feelings or point of view, this type of woman can brutally tell you to stop. "Shut up,"! The narcissist cannot handle the truth, and they make no effort to logically deny the other viewpoint.
- Curses! This is the last resort of narcissists and other bullies. If they cannot defend their position or behaviors, they resort to emotion-based personal attacks. It's another distraction

technique that deviates from the original point of the dispute by putting it on the defensive.
- Projection! They accuse and hold their victims responsible for actions or thoughts they have caused and are guilty of. This is a primitive defense mechanism. For example, I once heard a mother blaming her daughter for the birthday parties she had to do in childhood.
- Division! The narcissist sees the world as if it were all or nothing, right against evil, black and white. He has little ability to understand context or nuance. Either you see things her way, or you must be invalidated. You cannot agree and disagree with this kind of woman. Any criticism, the difference of opinion, or challenge to your authority is seen as a threat, and you will be treated in a devaluing and a demonizing way. This is another primitive defense mechanism.
- Prepare and attack! For a narcissist, discord or contempt is not enough. Everyone else in your world, including your own family and friends, should be hated and defeated for being wrong.
- Gaslighting! Women using this tactic deny things they have said and done (and often the victim of the same transgressions they have committed). They distort reality by stating that

the event never happened ... (you wondered ... you must be crazy) until you begin to doubt your own sanity ...

- Screams! There is no logic! The narcissistic and emotionally abusive woman, the more wrong she is, the more she will raise the tone of voice / or the more stubborn she becomes. Your level of false indignation, revenge, and emotional withdrawal is in direct proportion to the way you face you. She goes up, screaming, repeating the same simplistic, emotionally-charged statements until she drowns out the reason, or simply withdraws in ignorance until you send an apology for your "crime."
- Guilt and shame! The narcissists blames others for all that is wrong in their life and never consider how they themselves contributed to the situation or what their responsibility was, including whether they are unhappy; it was never their fault ... there is always someone to blame. They transfer the responsibility to make you look bad or crazy, still making an effort to be embarrassed and guilty in the end.
- They are unloading on the victim. When the narcissistic woman is placed against the wall or her dishonesty comes to light and cannot deny her, they turn around and throw the

justification and responsibility of their conduct on the victim. They claim that they have only reacted to aggression and are being unfairly attacked, so they have acted in "self-defense" because they always stand up for the truth, are the most honest, brave, and integral. They are practically illuminated!

Narcissism Characteristics in Men

The most significant difference between male and female narcissists is that they use their power differently.

Men are more inclined to exploit other people in order to gain more power themselves. They also find it reasonable that they are entitled to certain privileges.

Narcissistic men, in comparison with women, will have a greater tendency and desire to show their power. They show more leadership, dominance, and macho behavior.

Male narcissists are very focused on collecting money. With the money, they can gain control, status, and power and thus dominate others. Men don't care if they harm other people. The female narcissist likes spending money more.

The male narcissist always wants to win and show that he is better, whether this is at home or at work.

Other men are considered enemies. This way, even rivalry can arise between father and son.

The narcissistic father will also see his son or daughter as an extension of himself. Narcissistic behavior in men can quickly lead to physical aggression.

Both men and women display narcissistic characteristics because they want to escape from their pain. They are damaged people who were deeply traumatized in their past.

That is why they identify themselves with a personality that comes across as very confident, but nothing could be further from the truth. They feel very lonely deep down because they cannot make real connections with people.

Differences between Narcissism and Self-Esteem

David Levithan once said: "Narcissism. I couldn't believe I didn't have a full-length mirror." In fact, narcissism and self-esteem seek the legitimation of being. It is, therefore, easy to confuse these two terms. However, there are differences.

Where are these differences? Why do so many people confuse them so easily? It is simple: while narcissism pursues this search through a good image, self-esteem does it by simple existence, unconditionally.

Narcissism and self-esteem are opposite phenomena in the motivations and forms they generate. This is how two of the psychologists--Pilar Mallor and Manuel Villegas--who worked on this issue primarily think about.

In the research, they found clear differences between narcissism and self-esteem, although there are behaviors that can be attributed to both origins. In this way, how do we differentiate the two modalities in a person? Let's find out some points that clearly distinguish them.

- **The narcissist has an exaggerated perception of himself**

The main difference between the narcissistic person and the person with good self-esteem is the self-image. That is, the former gives it exaggerated and distorted importance. The latter has a much more interior, less inflated, and better-argued satisfaction.

That is, the narcissist seeks well-being and security through an exaggerated image, which, in reality, is a distorted self-perception. It shows a true inner void in which an insecure person hides.

For his part, a person with good self-esteem bases his well-being on satisfying relationships and does not give his image greater importance than it really has. Being a self-assured profile, you don't have to exaggerate or underscore successes ahead of others; simply enjoy them celebrating.

"Don't you think it's weird when someone has pictures of themselves everywhere? It's as if they're trying to prove they exist."

-Candance Bushnell-

- **Assertiveness against the need for attention**

A person with high self-esteem is assertive. He/she can listen, answer, and choose the moments to talk. In fact, it is done so knowingly and always placing value on its intervention. That is, it has emotional and social intelligence. In addition, you have the patience that gives you the confidence that when your turn comes, you may express your opinion.

However, the narcissistic profile, given its exaggerated image cult, needs attention. That is, it will always try to be the center of attention, letting everyone know that it is there. It needs constant worship of itself from others.

- **Empathy**

One thing that sets narcissistic people apart from the people with healthy self-esteem is their ability to empathize. This is precisely because the person with healthy self-esteem can develop in social interaction, the patience of which we speak, which is indispensable for active listening.

While a narcissist thinks only of himself and his image, a healthy self-esteem person is in a better position to connect with others. Because you don't have your attention occupied by the need to please, you can use it to put yourself in the skin of others. This will make it easier to understand different points of view, ideologies, and feelings.

- **Selfishness vs. cooperation**

Another key factor by which we can differentiate a narcissist from a person with healthy self-esteem is selfishness. It is easy to think that someone who thinks only of himself loves himself, but in reality, this projecting love is so full of doubt that it turns out to be his worst enemy.

While a person with high self-esteem knows when and how to show generosity and is accordingly cooperative, the narcissist is incapable. If you are not going to get a benefit, it will be hard to work hard.

"What makes the pain of jealousy so acute is that vanity cannot help endure it."

-Stendhal-

- **Arrogance vs. compassion**

Arrogance would be the fifth difference between narcissistic people and the people with healthy self-esteem. While the first group shows no compassion for anyone except perhaps for themselves, people who truly love each other have this virtue and know the beautiful feeling of helping others.

The narcissist, in his arrogance, is often aggressive, envious, and in need of dominance to feel good. He will hardly accept criticism, and however neutral it may be, he will tend to take it personally rather than for good. You will hardly learn from your mistakes, because you have great difficulty in perceiving them and, above all, in accepting them.

A narcissistic person and a person with healthy self-esteem may at first look very similar. However, as time passes and begins to give coherence to the two personalities, we see how this resemblance between narcissism and self-esteem vanishes like the mirage of water before an oasis.

CHAPTER 3

THESE ARE THE TRAITS THAT DEFINE THEM

Narcissism is one of the most studied personality traits in the field of psychology. When it occurs at very high intensity, it can cause mental disorders such as self-euphoric personality disorder, but even at low levels, it has impressive and sometimes conflicting properties.

We see the characteristics that define self-euphoric people and how they can be identified.

1. You are an unfair player

Burgo maintains that some narcissists are bullies and that one of their most problematic characteristics is the tendency not to know how to lose or win with grace. When these people lose a game, for example, they could try to humiliate the referee. When they win, they may over-indulge themselves or take on the losers.

2. You constantly feel undervalued

The kind of people Burgo calls "pompous" narcissists continuously complain about the world. Typically, they feel they deserve something better and think they don't get the recognition they deserve from others.

3. If you are not pompous, then you are introverted, hypersensitive, defensive and anxious

Psychologists speak of "two faces of narcissism." At the opposite, we find the super-aggressive and super-loud types in Donald Trump-style. However, there is also a milder form of narcissism. It is defined as "secret narcissism" and is characterized by introversion, hypersensitivity, anxiety, and being on the defensive. "Both sides of narcissism share a common basis of arrogance and a tendency to satisfy their needs at the expense of others," reports Scientific American.

4. You think everyone else is stupid

Many narcissists believe they know everything and find it difficult to get along with colleagues and friends as they refuse to think they can ever make mistakes about something. Burgo noted that these narcissists act with a strong sense of superiority over the others and that their decision-making approach is in the style "it is done as I say. Otherwise, that is the door".

5. You like to rail against others

Psychologists Nicholas Holtzman and Michael Strube of Washington University in St. Louis have discovered in a study that the most narcissistic subjects tend to be more controversial and to curse more than their modest counterparts. They also tend to use more sexually explicit language.

6. You are hypocritical

Narcissists are often convinced that their point of view is by its nature superior to that of others. But what really matters to them is the attention they receive when they defend their beliefs. For example, Burgo reports, a narcissist might believe he has a special relationship with God - but the thing that really matters is that others recognize this connection and admire his deep sense of spirituality.

7. You feel justified in being wrong with others

"Vindictive" narcissists usually know that vindictive or antisocial behavior is not acceptable. But they still feel right with their conscience acting in this way, because they always consider themselves victims of wrong, says Burgo. Moreover, these subjects often get offended for no reason, and therefore they are always told by others: "It's not what I meant!"

8. You like to command others and tell them what to do

Narcissists usually love leadership roles because they guarantee the ability to dominate others and satisfy their continuous need for positive reinforcements.

9. You are an entertainer

"A narcissistic monk would not be that great, while, on the contrary, being Kanye West and a narcissist is fantastic," said psychologist Peter Jonason of the University of Western Sydney, an expert in social psychology.

10. You are considered attractive, and you dress better than others

Narcissists usually tend to be more fashion-conscious and physically attractive, as evidenced by a study by Washington University psychologist Simine Vazire.

11. Betray in your relationships

Psychologists Joshua Foster of the University of South Alabama and W. Keith Campbell of the University of Georgia have discovered that narcissists are more likely to betray their partner once they know that this person is engaged with them. They also seem determined to convince others to take part in promiscuous sexual acts that they would not regularly participate in.

12. Do you like to humiliate people?

Narcissists intentionally humiliate others to keep their positive image high? In the long run, it becomes difficult because others do not applaud them anymore, so they must continue to seek new knowledge from which to obtain the next recognition. This also explains the reason why narcissists have only weak relationships.

13. Your parents ignored you or adored you

According to Sigmund Freud, the combination of refusal by parents with excessive admiration is more connected to adult narcissism than childhood, in which one of the two situations completely excluded the other. The incoherence and harshness of parents towards their children ultimately results in a "profound need for admiration" and causes narcissists to lead their lives in the constant search for what strengthens their ego.

14.Choose your friends to improve your image or take advantage of it

Narcissistic men and women have different ways of choosing their friends. Women want male friends with a high social status to feel valued. Men choose as friends of other men who can support them during their attempts to win girls.

15. You must always have everything under control

And exactly how they hate to talk about their feelings, "narcissists can't bear to depend on the decisions of others," says Malkin. "This reminds them that they are not invulnerable or completely independent - which they must ask to get what they want - and, even worse, which others may not want, to satisfy their demands." This is why they manage to control situations without getting angry. In the case of romantic relationships, narcissists control people with disapproving looks, call to warn of program changes, and are always late. This allows narcissists to undermine other people's decision-making possibilities. In doing so, narcissists maintain their sense of complete autonomy - what they desperately need.

Strategies to Protect Yourself from a Narcissistic Person

People with a marked narcissism not only stand out for that feeling of omnipotence and that highly swollen and unrealistic self-image. In addition, another aspect that most attracts attention to their personality is the way in which they relate to others, and how easily and spontaneously they generate discomfort in those around them.

And it is the belief strongly rooted in the narcissist that stands out above the rest of human beings is not something that is limited to remain isolated in his mind, without real consequences, but that predisposes him to act in a manner consistent with that vision of the world. That is why it is very common for narcissists to try to make others feel insecure, hesitant, and eclipsed by their real or imagined presence.

How to protect yourself psychologically from a narcissistic person?

These simple strategies can serve to mitigate the discomfort generated by certain frequent comments in people with high narcissism. However, keep in mind that these should be done so that a balance is maintained between your well-being and that of the other person.

You must keep in mind that partly being narcissistic is not an option; It is not, of course, for people with Narcissistic Personality Disorder, nor for those who, without reaching such clear extremes, have become accustomed to behaving in this way due to their past experiences and their socialization.

1. Cut the conversation

This is the most radical option, but also the simplest. There are situations that become so violent that withdrawal is a logical reaction. If you have the option, do it, and in many cases, this will have the effect of a kind of passive punishment such as the " time out " technique, in which the person who has behaved badly stops having access to something that was stimulating or entertaining.

2. Learn to recognize your feelings

In the face of offensive or contemptuous comments, it is useful to have good Emotional Intelligence. Experiencing a treatment characterized by the typical disdain of narcissistic people is not the same as going through that experience, considering that this situation is explained by the extreme personality trait of the person who pronounces those words. Thus, the possible harmful thoughts of self-esteem caused by the behavior of the other are relativized by the situation. What is happening does not talk about what the person is, but about the highly skewed thinking of the other person.

3. Remember that every human being has dignity

By default, every person has all the same rights, and all people are worthy. Whoever questions this principle is simply acting unilaterally, something that in fact, has no merit since, in any case, it shows an inability to socialize.

Disdain and teasing do not make one worthless, and they are a simple excuse to maintain that behavior and do not rely on the truth about what one is:

anyone can be mocked, but not everyone sees the need to articulate your social life through a feeling of superiority that must be fed artificially.

4. Don't reply in the same tone

Replicating in a similar way as the narcissistic person does when trying to be hurtful will only make the situation worse and longer. It is much better to contradict his speech (which usually consists of portraying the other person as immature or incapable) through fortitude, calm, and generally ignoring the presence of that person.

Once again, the key here is to eliminate the "reward" that would mean giving importance to the words of the narcissist and, by extension, to him/her as well.

5. Turn criticism around

If you reflect out loud on the criticisms of the other person showing that you had already reflected on them long ago and found a way to "deactivate" them, you will show unwavering security in you, and that will deter the other person from continuing. It is not necessary to explain why you think they are misguided (that would give them too much importance), just react in a way that shows that you are not shocked to hear those things.

Signs That You Are Raising a Narcissistic Child

Parents cannot neglect their children's self-esteem because healthy emotional development depends on it. However, so much importance has now been given to self-esteem that parents go beyond what is healthy and end up raising a narcissistic child.

A recent study of childhood egolatry revealed that parents who believe their children are better than other children do not help them develop a good self-esteem. On the contrary, they harm them and increase their risk of becoming narcissistic. This study concluded that in order to increase children's self-esteem, it is important that children feel loved, not feel better than others.

According to the researchers, when children are viewed by their parents as special and better children than others, they can internalize the view that they are superior, one that is centered on narcissism. But when children are treated with love and care by their parents, they internalize the idea that they are valuable people, a view that is the basis of self-esteem.

However, the overvaluation of parents is not the only factor determining narcissism. Like other personality traits, narcissism is also influenced by genetics and partly rooted in early temperamental manifestations.

Thus, due to their personality, some children are more likely to become narcissistic when exposed to an overvaluation of their parents.

How to realize if you are raising a narcissistic child

The following are clear signs that your educational practices are favoring the emergence of a narcissistic attitude in your child. Review and adapt these aspects so that your child has a healthier emotional and psychological development.

Let us not forget that, from a psychological point of view, narcissism is a personality disorder that has many negative connotations for people's lives, which ultimately suffer from it.

- **Make your child believe he is infallible**

Some children have difficulty believing in themselves; although they have sufficient skills to perform the tasks, they are paralyzed for fear of making mistakes. Increasing their self-esteem requires parents to support, praise, cheer, and convey confidence. Then they will realize that they are capable, which is worth a try.

It is one thing to praise, to acknowledge your successes, to let them trust your ability to solve problems, and quite another to make them believe that they will never go wrong.

Children need to learn to live with error; this is the best "medicine" for a narcissistic child. Error is part of life and learning. Not so when we learn to walk? Falling and getting up is part of learning. The one who makes mistakes is the one who lets himself try, who has the opportunity to succeed.

- **Compare your child with other children to show that he is superior**

From 7 or 8 years of age, children begin to compare with each other. Sometimes this interest in comparisons begins rather than being encouraged by parents, who are eager to show how good their children are or the qualities they believe they possess.

These comparisons create a lot of pressure on children who don't want to be left behind with their friends. When a child stands out, one must recognize his or her achievements and virtues, but without comparing them to others.

Being good or better at something doesn't mean being superior, but kids don't see it that way. Child's personality is in formation, and it is up to the adults to guide them correctly.

- **Offer the child a model unable to hear criticism**

Listening to criticism from others is very unpleasant for many adults, imagine for a narcissistic child. But we need to provide a model for children to accept constructive criticism. It is not a matter of bowing your head and saying yes to everything, but of accepting criticism, thinking about it, discussing the problem and committing to change, if appropriate.

Children learn by example. If they realize that their parents do not accept criticism that they are unable to change, that they act as if they are always right, they will do the same.

In addition, some parents do not accept their criticism of their children, react irrationally, and place their children on a pedestal of perfection and superiority.

- **Boast and excuse your shortcomings**

It is one thing to be proud of a child, and quite another to overvalue and excuse defects to prove that he is the best. Some children react by rebelling against their parents and others by feeding their narcissism. Neither option is an easy and healthy way for them.

From time to time, children "get their feet in their hands," but they don't have to be ashamed. Say sorry for your misbehavior, and show that we are not always perfect. The important thing is to learn from mistakes.

- **Speaking of different or "inferior" children**

A different or less capable child is not an inferior child. But if your child hears you criticizing such child for any reason, be it for an intellectual or physical disability or because he/she is dressed differently, the child believes he/she is superior to the child so discussed.

Often this negative way of talking about others is one way that one finds to be better than the other.

You don't have to show the worst of others for your best to appear. If a parent insists on bad-mouthing other children to make their child feel more important, all they can do is lose their true perspective about themselves, and they're worth it.

CHAPTER 4

THE LOVE BETWEEN AN EMPATH AND A NARCISSIST

Any relationship in which you cannot express your true feelings without worrying is meaningless.

1. The narcissist attracts empathy. They start a relationship. Empa's love is deep and unconditional. The narcissist, on the other hand, has no intention of developing or deepening the relationship, let alone establishing any affinity with the empath.

The empath is happy and content every time they are together, deluding themselves that their love is reciprocal.

2. The empath is convinced that he has finally met the love of his life. The narcissist convinces him by creating an illusion that makes the empath think that they have a special bond that will never break.

At times, it seems as though the narcissist is holding on to this relationship just as much as the empath, but this is a lie he gets himself into trying to deceive the other. The only thing the narcissist wants is to keep the other under control.

3. Over time, the narcissist will try to damage the empath's self-esteem by making him feel weak, insignificant, and incapable.

He will rarely attack him directly, but in any case, he will make comments such as, "Not that I want to offend you, but ...", after which he will point out some of the "flaws" of the empath. Like, "Not that I want to tell you what to do, but ..." if the empath doesn't do what it's asked for, then emotional harassment ensues.

4. The narcissist will become the sun, around which the empath will revolve since only the empath feels the love in this connection.

He will always try to help, understand, encourage, and reassure the narcissist. Will always be available to the narcissist when he needs it. The narcissist will try to put the halo on the martyr and the victim to manipulate the empyema to give him everything he needs.

5. The emp's intentions are pure. The empath has a good heart and cannot understand that the narcissist's wounds are different from his own, which is why their treatment is different.

The wounds of a narcissist cannot be healed with love, as the empath believes since they are immunized against it.

6. Everything in the relationship begins to revolve around the narcissist. Eventually, the empath begins to notice this, as, over time, he/she begins to feel scared to state and assert his/her desires and needs.

An empath will die rather than neglecting someone else for his/her own sake, even if he/she is not happy in the relationship that the narcissist brazenly takes advantage of.

7. The more affection, attention, and care the empath gives, the more the narcissist feels controlling.

And the more effort an empath makes, the more difficult it is to see that there is a problem. The trouble erupts when the empath finally wakes up and boils over to it.

8. At some point, the empath will get tired of being depreciated and depersonalized and will raise his voice. Empath feels devastated as his emotional needs are very frustrated.

When he realizes that he has lived in delusions all the time, he will start to tell aloud the truth about the state of affairs. The narcissist will not be happy about this turn of events.

9. A narcissist is someone who needs constant attention. It should be directed only to him. Feels pleased when people are obsessed with him.

But he is not capable of happiness anyway, no matter how much attention and praise he receives from others. There is always more to come. His thirst for attention is insatiable. The empath has a hard time understanding this.

10. When an empath starts talking openly about his feelings, the narcissist will quickly call him "crazy," "crazy," "too dramatic."

He will ignore any attempt by the emp to save the connection and try to manipulate him again to regain control.

11. It is impossible for an empath to understand such behavior. She will start blaming herself for all the bad things that happen in the relationship.

The narcissist has already convinced him that he is not "good enough" or that he has to try hard to earn his love.

12. Again, the empath does not realize that he has been manipulated. The narcissist has created a perverted version of reality in his mind.

The narcissist has led him to a state where he cannot

believe his own judgment, his own visions of things, and his own common sense.

Generally, it really starts to feel "crazy" and "crazy." This prevents him from realizing that the one who is "wrong" in the relationship is the narcissist.

13. Any attempt by the empath to communicate truthfully and honestly with the narcissist is doomed to failure. The narcissist will always project and transfer the blame to the other to justify himself because that is the only thing that interests him.

14. The empath must know that it is perfectly normal to feel confused, lost, defenseless, and deeply hurt. He needs to think seriously about his own personality and work on himself so that he can feel well again.

15. Empaths are the healers of society. They have the strength they need to overcome any challenge that comes their way.

They have the ability to ease other people's pain, make it their own pain.

16. The empathetic will know that he is a healer by nature. He has the inner strength to help others in the right way; sometimes he sees it as a duty, and sometimes life leads him to certain situations unexpectedly.

17. The empathetic person has to realize the bitter truth that not everyone deserves their love, care, and affection. Not everyone who seems distressed and unhappy is revealing his true self. There are some people who have sinister motives and have a very different view of relationships and people. You cannot trust someone who falls in love so quickly.

18. The moment when the empath realizes that the narcissist will never change is the moment of painful revelation and awakening.

This is the most important thing in this case, in order to be able to recognize and end this toxic link.

19. The narcissist will just continue with his lies. Nothing else will happen. He won't even remember the tremendous love and concern he was receiving.

20. The narcissist will continue to search for a new victim.

21. Empaths will become wiser, stronger, and much more considerate to whom they give love, time, and attention.

CHAPTER 5

SIGNS OF GASLIGHTING IN A NARCISSISTIC RELATIONSHIP

Gaslighting: the deadly game that the narcissist practices with his victims. Naming him and understanding the trap helps them get out of their confusion and escape.

Gaslighting is manipulating a person to question or question their own judgment or perception of reality, thus altering their emotional and psychological balance.

In general, narcissists apply this perverse game along with other tactics of emotional manipulation: denial, isolation, and selective memory, among others.

The narcissist during the entire relationship, from beginning to the end, subjected his victim, one way or another, some sort of gaslighting.

The abuser seeks, through this insidious method, to seize the victim's judgment and control his perception of himself and what is happening. The goal is simply to turn him into a puppet or fantoche to handle him at will.

In his purpose, he will spare no means; he will alter the environment, he will pretend not to have said what he said, he will use evasive and ambiguous language, he will categorically deny obvious facts, he will be falsely worried about the mental health of the person, he will be offended if the victim questions his claims, he will resort to third parties to convince the victim that something in her is not going well, day and night he will sow doubts about her abilities, make corrosive comments and emphasize her defects and errors.

It is an arsenal of mass destruction of enormous consequences for the emotional life and psychic balance of the person who suffers it. It is psychological violence in its purest form, whose consequences may persist even after the relationship has ended.

Abuse, although continuous, is perpetrated progressively and in a covert and subtle way. Only when the victim is able to relate the different situations experienced to each other does he realize the tremendous damage he has suffered? Unfortunately, this awareness often occurs when it is too late, and the effects of gaslighting are evident emotionally and psychologically.

Signs of Having Been Subjected or Suffering from Gaslighting

How to know if you have been a victim of gaslighting? How to identify the signs of this destructive control and conditioning tactic in time? Answering these questions is of vital importance in order to protect yourself from the deadly artillery of the narcissist, and start the path of recovery, for which it is essential, as will be said later, to break all contact with the person who applies this dangerous form of emotional and psychological manipulation.

Here are 10 signs that you may be, or have been, a victim of gaslighting:

1. The abuser takes advantage of the fears and vulnerabilities of the victim

The narcissist, who has studied the fears and weaknesses of the victim at the stage of love bombing, will use this knowledge in order to subject her to gaslighting by attacking her psychological and emotional defenses and making her feel inferior or vulnerable. For example, if he knows she is very anxious about her body weight, he will make negative comments so that she feels insecure about this aspect of her physical image.

Her fears of loneliness, failure, insecurities, all that is skilfully used by the manipulator to sow in the victim doubts about herself and her perception of reality.

2. The abuser acts as if he knew the victim fully

The abuser acts as if he was an omniscient narrator and knew in advance what the victim thinks and her way of being. He never qualifies his statements about her, but his judgments are always categorical. He is a specialist in putting labels on him and passing judgment on his actions. If she tries to defend herself or opposes him, he will say that she is lying or self-deceiving.

Sometimes he assumes a paternalistic or condescending posture, as if he was worried about the emotional health of the victim, or knew, without consulting her, what she needs.

3. The abuser will try to make the victim believe that they are "normal" situations that, in reality, are not

The narcissist will try to convince the victim that what she lives in the context of her relationship with him is perfectly normal and admissible, so she must accept it. If necessary, he will present some cases to prove that what he says is true.

Of course, its purpose is to condition the victim to assume clearly abusive situations as "normal". For example, in the face of "silent treatment," he will say that in all relationships, there are "silences," and he will accuse the victim of not understanding or not supporting him in his need to remain silent. Thus, "normalizing" a manipulative tactic as toxic and controlling as "silent treatment."

4. The abuser questions the sanity or judgment of the victim

If the victim reacts or complains about the situation of abuse he suffers, the narcissist will not only deny it flatly but will also strive to make the victim believe that he has lost his sanity or wit. He will say that he is paranoid, or too sensitive, or that he is overreacting, or that he is unbalanced, or that he is very dependent, etc.

All these expressions, which have a quite poisonous effect on the victim, seek to make him believe that the problem lies in him and in his perception.

5. The abuser gets the victim to start doubting himself

The narcissist, by force of denigrating her and invalidating her perception of the facts and of herself, makes the victim begin to have doubts about herself, about her judgments about reality, and even about her abilities.

Over time, the victim becomes an insecure and dependent person who anxiously seeks the approval of his abuser.

6. The abuser, given the reality of the victim, has a selective memory

The narcissist denies some facts and words spoken in the past. He will say, for example, that the arranged appointment was at a different time than the one agreed upon, making the victim believe that he is in error or that he simply figured it out. If the victim claims he will deny it without immutation and will be offended for doubting his word. All this generates confusion in the person who suffers it.

Another form of selective memory is the "forgetting" of certain important dates such as birthdays, anniversaries, etc. Instead, he perfectly remembers the failures and mistakes made by the victim at another time and brings them up even by taking them out of context.

7. The victim resorts to lying to avoid confrontation with the abuser

Although the person does not have the habit of lying, because of the stress he lives, he is able to pretend that he accepts the narcissist's point of view and that his perception agrees with his. Likewise, he will hide information for fear that it may be used against him by the abuser.

In this way, he avoids confronting the abuser, since each confrontation has devastating effects on his self-confidence and self-esteem, sinking him further into the nightmare of abuse.

8. The victim fears to communicate to others what she is living and isolates herself from others

The entire process of emotional and psychological erosion generated by gaslighting causes the victim to totally lose confidence in other people, so she tends to isolate herself and not communicate to others the ordeal she is going through.

Frequently, it is the narcissist himself who has deliberately promoted this isolation, cutting off possible ties of friendship and family that could serve as emotional and psychological support for his prey.

9. The victim questions her own mental and emotional sanity

Gaslighting completes its deadly arc when it makes the victim herself begin to doubt her own mental health and emotional balance. The brain-washing suffered has dramatically changed the perception she has of herself and has bowed submissively under the clutches of the evil narcissist.

At this point, the abuser has fully achieved his goal: the complete emotional and psychological destruction of the victim.

10. The victim presents a depressive picture

As the final consequence, the person experiences all the symptoms of depression: anxiety, lack of motivation, hopelessness, feelings of abandonment and loneliness, emptiness, frequent crying, etc.

The person feels without strength to react, loses vitality, and is as numb and dull.

CHAPTER 6

NARCISSISM IN RELATIONSHIP

The narcissism in the relationship is mediated by a person who at first dazzled us with his attention and captivating personality. However, later comes the true face and gimmicks that articulate fraud, manipulation, and emotional sabotage.

When narcissism arises in the relationship, anguish and fear appear as a result. Because far beyond what we may think, narcissistic men and women fall in love too. However, their mechanism of love generates a "rope" that knots around us. Every day tightens more, and every moment we lose more rights and wills and may have stolen our own voice.

Some claim to be a true "magnet for narcissists." Why does it happen? Is there any explanation why we cannot see this kind of profile and, therefore, cannot protect ourselves from it? Theories hold that, on average, it is the most sensitive and empathic people who are enchanted by this kind of personality.

There is perhaps a kind of feedback in which one nourishes the other's needs. However, it must be said that there is no conclusive data on this subject because, in fact, all of us, regardless of our being, age, or status, may be attracted to this profile. The reason for this lies in the fact that narcissists are often very magnetic at first and they are so well disguised that we cannot perceive their true self.

Thus, they often present traits such as great kindness, liveliness, a good sense of humor, intelligence, self-confidence, and shimmering extroversion that never go unnoticed. These 'superficial' attributes are irresistibly alluring for almost anyone. However, beneath this veneer stunning undoubtedly is the true skin, basically characterized by the inability to create a bond emotionally with someone positive.

Relationship narcissism: tips on how to act

The way narcissism in the relationship arises can be distinguished in different realities. Thus, it is common for two very specific facts to occur: the first, that narcissism comes from both members of the couple.

The second that it is one of the two who is clearly and evidently engaging in a behavior as harmful as it is destructive to one's relationship. These are undoubtedly two situations that we must analyze.

Narcissism in Relationship: When Both Act Selfishly

It is important to differentiate narcissistic behavior

from a narcissistic personality disorder. In the latter case, we would be talking about a clinical condition provided for in the Diagnostic and Statistical Manual of Mental Disorders (DSM-V).

Therefore, it may be the case that in a relationship, two people are involved with this personality type or even with this disorder. It is unusual, but it can happen. At the same time, another reality that sometimes happens in the life cycle of a relationship is as follows:

- We set aside the couple's needs to prioritize ours.
- It is not just this emotional neglect that arises. In addition, certain behaviors appear, such as the need for control and the good and bad times when we sometimes want our partner around, and sometimes we want distance.

What is the explanation for this kind of relationship? What happens when relationship narcissism comes from both members? What happens is that this bond lies in an abyss in which, sooner or later, it will come to an end. There are couples who have ceased to love each other and yet are unable to take the next step towards a healthy end.

Signs That Your Partner Is Narcissistic

A narcissistic partner will end up making you feel that you are inferior. Although at first, they are great conquerors, when the game is over, they may make you feel guilty, belittled, and undervalued.

Narcissism is commonly used as a negative character trait - a way of suggesting that someone is self-conscious or not considered by others. Unfortunately, real narcissism is much more than that!

People with a narcissistic personality disorder can be very detrimental in relationships and can severely damage their partners' self-esteem.

And if you're dating someone who is a narcissist at first, you might be impressed by your self-confidence and your aura of grandeur and grandeur. But as the relationship progresses, you will soon realize that the more perfect they claim to be, the more they begin to embarrass you. And the only way to please this person or get into your good books is to be ashamed and feel worse about yourself. Now really, can this be healthy for you??!

Narcissistic personality

According to psychologist Stephen Johnson, a narcissist is a person who "has buried the true expression of himself in response to early wounds, and has replaced it with a false, highly developed, compensatory self."

Therefore, the traditional image of the narcissist in love with himself is not the image that corresponds to the real narcissist. On the contrary, the narcissist is not in love with himself, much less, but is in love with the idealized image that he has made of himself.

In reality, they are deeply injured people with low self-esteem, who hide under an idealized self so as not to face reality. It is not easy to deal with a narcissist. In fact, his need to feel a superior and idealized being can even lead him to belittle and underestimate the other.

Obvious Signs You're Dating a Self-Obsessed Narcissist

1. Your conversation is not a conversation

Having a conversation with a narcissist can become an infinite weariness, a really frustrating experience. This is so because, in reality, the narcissist does not "talk," but maintains an endless and tedious monologue. It is not a dialogue, and there is no exchange.

In fact, even if you try to take the floor with some "good," "well," "really," it won't allow you to participate. And this because the narcissist knows everything and better than anyone. Your comments, if you manage to express them, will be ignored or corrected. They love to have listeners, not the interactive ones.

For this reason, it is normal for you to feel really frustrated after trying to talk with a narcissist.

2. The conversation revolves around "me, me, me and me too"

The topic of conversation will always end up revolving around himself. In fact, even in conversations with more people, he will always try to take the turn to return the conversation about himself. For this reason, narcissists are people who constantly interrupt, taking the turn of speech without respecting others.

In addition, not only do they not listen to others, but they end up ignoring them and monopolizing any evening. For this reason, if your partner is a narcissist, it is logical that you feel belittled and undervalued and it is inevitable.

3. He likes to break the rules

The narcissist needs to feel different and superior. For this reason, it is common for narcissistic people to enjoy breaking some rules. For example, not respecting some traffic rules, taking home office supplies, etc.

These actions make them feel that they are above the rules, laws, and society. They feel they are unpunished and superior. So they like going the odd way.

4. You're dating a narcissist and don't respect the limits

As superior, you are below. For this reason, the narcissist will not respect you, nor attend to your needs. He is the priority. Have you asked for money and never returned it? Does he show pride in your feelings or achievements, belittling them? So, maybe you're dating a narcissist.

5. Project a false image of yourself

It is the basic external characteristic of the narcissist. They spend too much time getting ready, for example, because they have to impress others. In addition, they usually even take pride in front of others: "Look how good this feels," "look how special I am."

Indeed, they must create the idea in others that they need to be admired. However, in reality, they are deeply insecure beings with low self-esteem.

6. They must be the center of your world when you're dating a narcissist

Not only are your needs less important, the narcissist expects you to cover his/hers preferentially. In the couple, the narcissist considers that he/she is the most prominent element of the couple, so he/she will require that you pay attention at all times, without considering your needs and obligations.

7. At first, it was lovely

When he tried to conquer you, it was lovely. You saw a charismatic and persuasive, charming, and thoughtful person. However, as the relationship progressed and interest in the conquest disappeared, you were relegated to second place.

The narcissist must be the best in everything. Therefore, he must also be an ideal conqueror. Once he is bored with the game, things are very different.

8. If you're dating a narcissist, he's an exceptional hero

By feeling superior, he creates an idealized image of himself that he believes to be true. Indeed, he presents himself as a hero or heroine, someone extremely exceptional and superior to others. For this reason, he will be convinced that you are nothing without him. His sense of superiority seeks the annihilation of your self in front of him.

9. Some narcissists are victims

A good way to get the attention of others is to present yourself as a victim. This way, they will get you to forget your needs and focus on them. Their goal from the beginning.

However, this can also happen at any time. The narcissist is often "alluded to" constantly so that he feels guilty about how you treat him if he is not what he wants to be.

10. Is a manipulator

The others are nothing more than something or someone to use to meet their needs. For example, they can choose a partner who is a really beautiful person physically only to show others certain status.

How to act if you are dating a narcissist

If you want things to change, you have to be more assertive. Therefore:

- First, show that it bothers you. In fact, you should imply the things that bother you, such as not being able to have a conversation, that your needs are always the priority, etc. Talk to him that you are also important and have your own needs and demands.
- Stay positive even when explaining to the narcissist that you also exist; you should do it in a way that he cannot understand that such a situation bothers you too much. Indeed, if you express yourself as really angry, you may even

be reaffirming their superiority, as if they were right.
- Stay focused. Although the narcissistic person tries at all times to make you see that he and his goals are more important, remember that you also have yours. Do not get carried away, and do not forget that you also have personality, needs, goals, and dreams.
- Recognize that this person needs help. If you want to continue with the relationship, it is important that you understand that the narcissist, deep down, is an insecure person with low self-esteem. Perhaps, in this sense, you can even help him.

Things You Can Expect in a Relationship with a Narcissist

1. Expect narcissists to feel more right than their counterparts.

Narcissists are extremely self-centered and selfish. They are focused on their own needs, so they have difficulty thinking about someone else unless they are forced to. They will take the last piece of bread, even if it means someone will be left without. The balance is always biased towards them, always receiving more than their share. They feel entitled to receive without giving the same in return because, in their minds, it will be unfair if they receive less. And they often display childish tantrums, but with adult words, when they don't get what they want. You can expect to give more than you get in this relationship, because they may never have learned how to share or commit, so there will always be inequality.

2. Do not expect to see any empathy.

Most narcissists are unable to have compassion. Empathy is not a natural trait they exhibit. They find it impossible to put themselves in someone else's shoes or sympathize with what someone might be feeling. They do not feel their pain as empathic people do. They often diminish, ignore, or even get angry when someone is expressing feelings openly. There is an instant reaction rather than listening because they feel attacked, especially when it has nothing to do with them, as such situations put the other person in focus and not them.

3. Do not expect to hear the truth.

Many narcissists are habitual liars and lack integrity. To tell the truth about themselves would mean that they would have to humiliate themselves or expose everything they are trying to hide. They prefer to be deceptive than to be truthful. Even in the face of ordinary people, like many others, they want to impress and pass a good image. They will say they are nice people, not the bad people they really are, or they will talk about all the great things they have ever done in their lives. They paint a beautiful self-portrait that everyone should admire. If you question lies or try to expose the truth, you can expect to get more lies and/or narcissistic anger.

4. Expect to see anger.

A narcissist is like a big bully and at the same time, a child when he is not getting what he wants, not getting the attention he wants, or having his integrity questioned anyway. They hope to be reliable even after many lies. And they do not accept any kind of criticism, even if it is uttered in the gentlest way. Nor do they want to hear about the past or what they have done, even if they have never apologized for it. Their expectations of others are very high, while their expectations of themselves are low. Then, when you do not live up to their expectations, you will see annoyance and disappointment as anger.

If you start to see the pattern (the cycle of abuse) and try to get their attention, you'll get the anger as everything you've ever done is thrown at you as if you were to blame - which makes you defensive, instead of getting to the problem. They cannot hear you or accept the truth. Everything must be your problem, and they don't want to hear from you. This anger is very dangerous - be very careful and seek help in this situation.

5. Expect to be controlled with manipulation.

Narcissists are great at using mind games to manipulate people into getting what they want. If they are not using anger to manipulate, they are using their charm. They use money, rewards, or whatever they have to get what they want or to convince them of an alternative story. Another way to keep lies hidden is to use a psychological tactic called gaslighting. This tactic is used to make you feel confused and wonder if your brain is right about something that happened or was said. The narcissist will deny and try to convince you that they know better than you about what happened - they didn't say that you heard it wrong, etc. You begin to doubt yourself and wonder if you are going crazy (he or she may even call you that) when, in fact, all the time, you are being manipulated.

6. Expect the narcissist to need tons of positive admiration.

The narcissist is fuelled by the admiration of others. Their language of love is words of wonder, and often they are in competition for it. They repeatedly tell stories (often exaggerated or lying) to make people think big things about them. The stories can be stories of heroes, military achievements, or sporting achievements (the best football player on the team) because the narcissist knows that people admire a hero or a highly successful person. Narcissists are often successful on their own because they are charming and have an inflated sense of self-esteem. But he or she thinks he is better than everyone else and deserves to be the person at the top and in charge, even if he or she doesn't deserve it.

7. Expect to see both sides of this person.

When dealing with a narcissistic person, you will begin to see that the lamb is actually the disguised wolf - the sheep-skin wolf. Telling your stories and lies to pretend to be someone you do not mean they have a reputation or image to protect. With the undercover narcissist, the outside world sees a caring person who is very different from his true character behind closed doors.

The bombardment of love is one of the narcissist's secret weapons to attract their next relationship. Bombardment of love means overwhelming someone with attention and affection for the sole purpose of locking them into a relationship. A narcissist will profess love to someone he or she barely knows - you are suddenly "soul mates" because of a physical attraction. Faced with compromise, the truth about the narcissist will be revealed. This is his true character, being cool just to get what he wants, but only until the purpose is served.

8. Expect them to be serial adulterers or sex addicts.

Although women may be narcissistic, and they also commit adultery, men are more likely than women to exhibit narcissism. This is probably most evident when they exchange their wives for a lover or become sexually ill (addiction to excessive pornography, rapists, child molesters, etc.).

Narcissists have no self-control and are never happy. They may also have addiction problems, or their lack of contentment makes them look for more and more of the things that give them pleasure. They often walk out of their current relationships when they run out of supplies of constant admiration that the other person can give them. And because they are filling a need in their own lives, they do not apologize or feel bad about what they have done.

9. Expect to be the primary caregiver.

Many narcissists are unable to be alone, so they jump from relationship to relationship, often securing new relationships to make sure they have someone in the background. They do not take time alone to understand why they need a caregiver, constant admiration, and someone to blame. Narcissists look for people who are "servants" or "repairers" because they know that such people always take on the burden of responsibility and fulfill all their needs. With your unmet needs, you can feel very lonely in this relationship because they don't need partners but admirers.

CHAPTER 7

HOW NARCISSISTS MANIPULATE THEIR VICTIMS

Until you meet the narcissus, you can't even imagine how convincingly he can play the victim.

His goal is to subtly manipulate you so that you do what is beneficial to him without being aware that this is happening. This is where the ability to play the victim comes in handy.

Learn ways narcissus tries to play the victim and how to prevent him:

1. Lies

This is the first trick that narcissus resorts to during the confrontation. He just lies in the living eyes.

Narcissus hopes to reject your arguments and disarm your skepticism. It will make you think something has happened (which actually didn't happen) or agree that it looked completely different.

When you agree to recognize this lie - the narcissus wins again.

Unfortunately, I have committed this sin many times. I waved my hand because "maybe he really thinks it was like that?" or "he was so sweet," or "I don't want to argue, I prefer peace."

If you know you are being lied to, or have that impression, don't give up. Trust your gut feeling and don't take shortcuts, because narcissus counts on that. Reject his lie, disagree with his version, show any evidence that he is fabricating false facts.

Yes, it can be a long and unpleasant discussion, because he has not been born yet, who would prove something to a narcissist, but it is important that he receives a clear signal from you that you are not buying a lie. It will deter him gradually.

He will continue to play the victim and try another trick somehow.

2. Gaslighting

As mentioned before, Gaslighting is a good buddy of lies because narcissus often reaches for gaslighting right after he tried to twist the truth. It is defined as manipulation that is intended to cause the victim to doubt or question whether what he knows is the truth and reality in which he lives.

Gaslighting is very difficult to spot at the moment. The best defense known is that you can experience it during a conversation. As with lies, don't agree to its "version." Don't give him satisfaction, and don't start questioning your truth.

Gaslighting resistance is a real blow to narcissus.

When you learn this, you will take away some confidence and will start to be a bit of a rush in your manipulations.

The most destructive gaslighting was done by two people: my daughter's father and my mother. It took me decades to recover, and I still couldn't get back to myself. I can only wonder who I would be today if I had not been taught to question my sanity, my choices, and my judgments.

Every mistake I made later only strengthened their doubts.

My mother could play a victim accusingly. To this day, I am haunted by the sight of her lying on the couch, in a green dressing gown, with a wet towel on her head (that is, I led her to a terrible headache) and sometimes the hateful looks of her stepfather and sister (so-called flying monkeys, about which I will still write) , because my mother "Because of me" she took too many sleeping pills.

As a child, of course, I didn't have a chance to defend myself against gaslighting. That's why then my ex could manipulate me freely and play a victim.

3. Change of history

If the lie and gaslighting fail, the narcissus will simply try to change the story. Maybe not all, but small details - what did he say, what did you say, what happened. The idea is to force you to defend, and then calmly implement strategy number one and two.

Again, in order not to let the narcissus play the victim, you must stick to the truth, you know, which is true and do not let him change this situation. When he understands that he is not able to convince you of his distorted version of events, he will start to attack eventually.

4. Projection

Narcissus already knows that you won't let yourself lie; you don't feel like gaslighting, and you don't accept a version of events other than the one that really took place.

What else can narcissus do to continue playing the victim? A healthy person would accept the situation, but the narcissist will not feel that he is doing something wrong. He will try to reverse the role in the style "what about ...?!".

If the narcissus starts attacking you, bring the discussion back to the right track saying, for example: "I would like to talk about how I made you feel this way, but now I would like to focus on the subject and tell you my truth about what happened."

Don't let yourself be defensive so that you suddenly have to defend yourself.

5. Offensive

The final stage of the narcissus playing the victim is the transition to the offensive. Most often, a very offensive phase, and it is difficult to counteract it.

Narcissus entering the offensive wants to completely destroy your self-esteem and leave you as an emotional wreck. He will do and literally say anything to achieve his goal.

How to react to a narcissus on the offensive? Most importantly, don't let this offensive action work on you. Keep calm and confident, looking boldly in his eyes, do not let him play the victim.

Outsmarting a narcissist who plays the victim is not easy, but not impossible; you can. However, if at some point, you start to fear for your safety, run and take shelter where a narcissus fails to hurt you.

Things You Shouldn't Do In Dealing with Narcissists

We need to apply different rules in our communication with people who suffer from narcissism. Here are 11 things to do when dealing with them:

Don't take them for "pure coin." The image is all about narcissists. They work hard to build a facade of excellence and confidence. They like to make others guess and therefore maintain a state of opacity. However, it is important to remember that people suffering from narcissism are deeply insecure. Their shiny facade is designed to hide the void inside. We may have compassion for their pain, but not be misled by their claims. Not everything that shines is gold, after all.

Do not share too much personal information. The more personal information you give to a narcissist, the more enmity he receives against you. Narcissists always need to be on top. They can use anything you share to humiliate or manipulate you, especially when you are most vulnerable or in need. Be reasonable about what you tell them. Confide with extreme caution.

Do not feel obligated to justify your thoughts, feelings, or actions. Many narcissists try to cast doubt on the other. They can do this by asking sharp and leading questions, as if you owe them an explanation. Accept it as it is, an attempt to undermine your personality. One useful self-help mantra is "No CCF," which means "No Excuse, Controversy, Defense or Explanation." You do not need to explain or justify your feelings or thoughts. In addition, arguing or defending yourself against a narcissist is usually counterproductive. Narcissists tend to be interested in winning the battle, not listening or communicating.

Don't downplay their dysfunctional behavior. Narcissistic behavior and hunger for attention can drain the energy of the people around them. As a result, over time, they are so exhausted or numb that they cannot record how unhealthy narcissistic behavior is. Don't be fooled: cheating, manipulation, and humiliation are unhealthy and wrong. Sometimes it may be best to leave the narcissist's childish or provocative behavior without comment, but that doesn't mean you shouldn't make a mental note of how unhealthy all this is.

CHAPTER 8

THE DIFFERENCE BETWEEN SELF-ESTEEM AND NARCISSISM

The thin line between self-esteem and narcissism

In short, narcissism is self-esteem raised to the maximum power, the excessive admiration you feel for your physical appearance, qualities, or gifts.

Self-centeredness, related to the above (although not exactly the same), is the paranoia of the narcissist; the admiration you feel for yourself is such that you believe you are the center of all other people's attention and concern.

These two psychological phenomena seem to describe what happens to many people, but for those who are not familiar with the subject, it is good to highlight the differences between narcissism and self-esteem.

The difference between narcissism and self-esteem is that the former implies the denial of the value of others, which are reduced to mere providers of attention and fame. Self-esteem, on the other hand, is what makes us feel good about ourselves as beings integrated into a society full of perfectly valid human beings with a due regard to the feelings of others. But... does not the passage of time transform our self-esteem into narcissism through the use of new technologies?

The evolution of narcissism

Adolescence is a stage of the revolution, among other things, hormonal, which leads us to have ups and downs of self-esteem. Hopefully, after this time, we will have managed to leave it unharmed and with a level of regular self-esteem.

This set of perceptions, thoughts, and assessments of ourselves will undoubtedly affect how we see the world around us. According to some theories, we build our self-esteem based on the social acceptance of our peers. But there comes a time when someone's ego, perhaps ours, is greatly inflated and stands out; He loves himself excessively and considers himself superior to everything else.

The cult towards the ego

The cult of ourselves, the body, or the mind, according to the time, has existed since long ago.

Let us start from the narcissistic word itself that comes from the myth of Narcissus, existing in both Greek and Roman mythology. It speaks of a handsome young man who stole the heart of every woman and who, because he angered who should not, ended up drowning in the water for being in love with his own reflection.

The problem exists; therefore, since ancient times, what has changed are the elements of the game. He has given us the "selfies," get many "likes," have many photos, and many friends, followers...

Probably everyone, in one way or another, sometimes sins of having the ego primed. However, it is easier to see the straw in another's eye.

Actually, the only thing we can blame on the Internet is that it has made it easier and more universal. Now I can boast of having a lot of friends without having to work or take care of those relationships, having a "like" from time to time. I can teach others, my hundreds of "friends," how happy I am with my life, my partner, my work, how handsome I am to the natural (with mobile applications that correct you, increase, decrease and cover, of course). In short, it is easy because I choose what to show. Fabrication has become easier now.

The reality is that we live in a frantic era of capitalism and a liberal economy, where we confuse happiness with consumerism, and this is consuming us. Even so, the possibility of crossing the line of self-esteem to self-centeredness and narcissism existed before any social network. If not, ask Donald Trump; that is a good example of what it is to love yourself in excess.

The neural circuits of egocentrism

Internally, these small moments of pseudo-happiness that grant us too much adoration and make it known on the networks activate the brain reward center as well as sex, eating, generosity...

And, after all, what gives meaning to our existence, what moves and motivates us from the most biological and basic point of view, is reward and pleasure. How we get it will continue to vary: it is now fashionable to pose in photos and put a filter on my pasta dish, but perhaps hopefully, tomorrow, we will try altruism and generosity as a mechanism of cerebral reward.

We must take care of the "child" that we carry inside, but that does not mean cramming it with candy.

Tricks That Narcissus Uses To Lower Your Self-Esteem

A relationship with a narcissist is the slow death of your self-esteem. Narcissus loves to deprive his victims of strength because, in this way, he feels better.

Such people are both mean and extremely attractive. They are charming to such an extent that you can't even think about it that under this attractive surface lays a nasty personality. Sweet poison, in actual.

Imagine a beautiful, red, and juicy apple, full of ugly worms inside. This is exactly what a narcissus is.

That is why most people who were lucky and did not know the narcissus before, think that they are not harmful. They don't notice the danger, they leave the proverbial guard, and then bam! Narcissus attacks.

You may not even realize that you are in the company of a narcissist - a partner or even a parent.

The longer you stay in the company of narcissus, the more he tries to lower your self-esteem. And then he can feel his superiority.

They change the world around them into a negative and ugly place that perfectly reflects their nasty soul.

Do you know the story of a slowly cooking frog? Well, this is how the process of destroying the self-esteem of a narcissist victim looks somewhat.

Here is what they most often say to achieve their goal:

1. You are just oversensitive

Narcissus can use any violence - both emotional and physical - then you realize that maybe it's time to escape. However, before this happens, the narcissist's victim tries to naively confront him with his behavior, give him gentle attention.

If you do this, the narcissus will immediately turn the cat's tail and begin to blame you for an exaggerated reaction to his 'right' and 'sensible' behavior. My favorite text is, "but what do you mean."

Narcissus will hurt you and manipulate you, but if you pay attention to him, you will find out that you are oversensitive.

2. Does everything have to revolve around you?

The only person who is worried about and takes over the narcissus is himself. If you try to talk to him about how you feel - even though you are going through an incredibly difficult time, he does not care at all.

So if you accidentally tell them what you expect, they will accuse you of selfishness and thinking only about yourself.

Everything must always revolve around them. Try to express even the slightest expectation; they will immediately direct attention back to you.

3. You are insecure/ jealous

As a seemingly charming person, narcissus is very happy to flirt. Maybe he will never betray you, but you will never feel a sense of security with him.

He will flirt to make you jealous, to trigger the right response.

He wants you to try harder, but he doesn't have to strain.

Narcissus loves attention, so he will take advantage of every opportunity when it seems attractive to someone.

Try to remind him, and you will find out that you are insecure and jealous.

4. You are crazy!

One of the worst forms of manipulation that narcissus uses is the so-called gaslighting, i.e., bringing about a situation where you start to question your mental health.

He attacks your personality (you are oversensitive), denies everything you accuse him of, and makes you feel (and often behave yourself) as if you were actually crazy.

There is no truth about the narcissus, the network of manipulations, lies, and subject changes means that you no longer know what reality looks like.

Narcissus knows what button to press (and does) to provoke you until you respond.

And then calmly observes your (hysterical, of course) reaction, you do exactly what he expected so that he could call you crazy and mentally unstable.

5. Who will believe you?

Narcissus not only tries to destroy your faith in yourself, but also the faith of others in you. Complains to other people, they use your sensitivity as an argument against you and proof of how hard their life with you is. Isolating the victim and making him more vulnerable serves the interests of the narcissist.

Narcissus will spread rumors about you, systematically alienating you from loved ones and friends. And when it leads to the fact that you will be alone and begin to doubt yourself, it will cease to hide from anything, glad that it destroyed you without being discovered. The narcissist often succeeds in his vicious propaganda.

CHAPTER 9

NARCISSISTIC ABUSE CYCLE

The Narcissistic Abuse Cycle is a cycle of manipulation and abuse that can also be applied to people who live or lived with people with a Type B personality disorder (DSM-IV). These disorders are as follows:

1. Narcissistic Personality Disorder

2. Histrionic Personality Disorder

3. Borderline Personality Disorder (Borderline)

4. Antisocial Personality Disorder (Sociopath)

All Group B personality disorders, although they are different from each other, have many similarities in their behaviors and attitudes. The volatile self-esteem of the narcissist is constantly looking for a narcissistic supplement to feel important and validated by the people around him.

Narcissists feel constantly threatened inside and are not anchored to reality. They feel very insecure, and it is for this reason that they constantly create chaos to receive attention and love.

The Narcissistic Abuse Cycle in Relationships
Idealization phase. When the relationship between the Narcissist and the Victim begins.

Love bombing: The narcissist fills the victim's attention, opens contact with her every day, and this lasts for hours. It fills him with flattery and attention, it seems like happening suddenly and almost out of nowhere and without knowing much, and the connection turns out to be huge and unstoppable.

Hurry towards intimacy: The narcissist will tell you very personal things about his and his life very quickly, too. In phases in which the people he talks about are tastes and hobbies, the narcissist will tell you about very intimate things (his divorce, a traumatic event of childhood, the relationship with his mother). They do this so that you do the same, so they have a lot of information about you and make you trust them very quickly. Moreover, they are interested in your weaknesses.

Listening/offering personal support: They will listen to you very carefully in a way that you have seen a few times; they are available to you at all times to support you in everything you need. Have you quarreled with a friend? They will give you their wise advice. Have you had a bad day at work? They will give you their shoulder to cry if you need it. You will be the focus of the attention of their lives for a period of time. The fervor last only until they win you over completely.

Make "mirroring" in a false way: They will make your "mirror" so that it seems that you are soul mates. If you like riding, they have long wanted to try it, and if you are a romantic, they will prepare a scene for you to "Memories of Africa," if your dream has always been to travel to Peru and see the Machu Picchu, what chance! The narcissists are just that.

Hyper-sexuality: Many of them are very good at sex, especially somatic narcissists (soma means body in Greek). They will want to know what you like in bed, what makes you have orgasms; they will display enormous creativity and wealth in this area. They will do this not only because they enjoy sex immensely but because they are aware that sex is a huge hook in a relationship, and after this phase, they will use it to control and dominate you.

Devaluation phase. This can occur openly in front of the Victim or covertly behind their backs.

If it happens behind their backs, nothing bad will happen to the victim until they are discarded.

Walking on embers: The victim will feel that he has to walk on embers with everything he says or does as if at the minimum it was possible to actuate a button that aroused the anger, contempt, rejection, of the narcissist. The relationship has literally become a minefield for the victim.

A streak of narcissistic anger, which may or may not include various types of abuse: verbal, physical, emotional, psychological, sexual, spiritual, or financial.

Cheating the victim with third parties (Triangulation): This usually occurs during all phases of the relationship, but it is at this stage when the narcissist lets him see in a more obvious way: messages on Facebook to other people, hide the phone, they are supposed to meet friends but then it turns out that they met their ex and went to drink with him/her.

Pathological lies: Narcissists lie a lot; it is part of the psychological game of creating confusion around you. The lies can range from something innocent and absurd, such as lying about the fact that they had a dog as a pet in childhood that doesn't really exist or talk about that year they spent Erasmus in Italy. You just discover that he has never lived in Italy.

Parasitic way of life: The narcissist begins to take advantage of the victim financially (this regardless of the situation that the narcissist wins five times more than the victim), to pay more of the household expenses, by chance your card runs out of funds constantly, you lose your job and don't seem to be in a hurry to find another one.

The narcissist uses small tactics to make the victim doubt himself, phrases like "Sometimes our friends think you are very childish," "no, you didn't leave the keys there, I think sometimes your head goes away, "you get hysterical, I think you're bipolar. "

The victim begins to question her behavior and herself: is he/she or is it me? I have a problem? Am I exaggerated/dramatic/ hysterical?

Discard Phase

On/off button in the relationship: The narcissist will leave the victim overnight, without warning and leaving the victim very surprised and bewildered. It is as if the narcissist, instead of normal emotions, had an on and off button with respect to the relationship and the victim (I love you vs.you do not exist).

Silence treatment: It is a form of psychological abuse through which the narcissist closes all forms of communication with the victim. If they did not do it before in the devaluation phase (very likely), they will do so in this one, to increase the desire of the narcissist at some point to contact again in the future.

Absence of closure: With a narcissist, there is never a concrete closure because they do not allow it. If he/she leaves the relationship, he will do so without explanations or goodbyes, or a dignified closure that honors the relationship you have had. Later (months, sometimes years later), it is very likely that the narcissist will try to contact you again by hovering (a technique with which they try to resume contact with them) to test whether you can be a possible target again.

The mask of the Narcissist is removed: In this phase, the narcissist reveals his true personality and usually shows a huge lack of empathy and regrets. Frequently, from one day to the next, photos are uploaded to social networks with their new partner, explaining to the four winds how happy they are and how in love they are as if the relationship with the victim had never existed.

Of course, it is also possible for the victim to leave the narcissist. In this case, the narcissist is likely first to try that the rupture does not occur with all kinds of lies, manipulations, and strategies. If this occurs equally, it will disappear by applying the silence treatment. The chances are very high of reappearing after weeks, months, or even years without contact, trying to get the victim to return to his / her relationship or become a secondary source of narcissistic supplement. He will try this through the technique known as "hovering."

CHAPTER 10

REASONS WHY NARCISSISTS CANNOT INTIMATE RELATIONSHIPS

The Narcissism and Narcissistic Personality Disorder is defined as "a great sense of grandiosity, lack of empathy for others, and a constant need for admiration."

Narcissists need to feel a certain level of power and superiority over others. In what can be described as a superficial "social circle," they only interact with people who believe they have a certain status and consider them special. In a more intimate circle, they surround themselves with people to whom they feel superior. The interesting thing is that they exhibit an aura of self-confidence -- a characteristic that makes some people feel attracted to them that in reality, is a mask. Most are actually very fragile people.

The rules of a normal relationship cannot be applied to any relationship with a narcissist because it is not normal in any sense. Narcissists will take advantage of your acts of kindness, your vulnerabilities; they will look for what they consider weaknesses to exploit for their own benefit.

A narcissist cannot have an intimate relationship simply because of the way he interacts with others prevents him from having that kind of connection with another human being.

These are the reasons.

Reasons why Narcissists cannot Intimate Relationships

- **They don't trust others**

In an intimate relationship, the two people show their vulnerability, and this requires trust. Can someone with Narcissistic Personality Disorder trust a partner? No, they can't. This is related to their inability to empathize with others and a fierce fear of showing themselves to others as they really are, which unconsciously leads them to close completely emotionally. They are emotionally inaccessible, so a relationship with a narcissist is not really a relationship, but a game of power, control, and domination. They only seek the gratification of their irresistible and infinite need for admiration.

- **They always look for something in return**

To placate his insatiable hunger for domination, power, and control, the narcissist will victimize his partner, and he will not think twice.

At first, they will give only to later remove it: affection, love, tenderness, time, money, and admiration. There is a huge display of attention to give, but all that giving is not authentic or selfless, it has a price. After the first phase of idealization, they will begin to take it off, seeking to devalue you as a person. It is a game in which they always want to win. All of that they give is a bait to allure you.

The key is that Narcissists want something (love, sex, shelter, money, and/or admiration), not someone.

- **They are experts in looking for dead angles**

Narcissists are like predators that are always behind something, and they have a goal. They do not see people as independent beings but as extensions of themselves, as potential suppliers of the narcissistic supplement, which is what they "feed" on to exist.

Because of this, they are experts in detecting the weaknesses of others and then being able to press the appropriate buttons to get the victims serve their goal. If you currently suspect that you interact with a narcissist, observe his/her behavior. He will try to get a lot of information about you very quickly, to know what your "dead angles" are, what are those buttons that will make you jump as if you had a spring that makes you reactive. That is what they will seek to exercise control and domination over you. They utilize the vulnerabilities of the victim to achieve their goal, that is, to exercise exclusive and absolute control over his/her being.

- **Your behavior ALWAYS ends up being abusive**

It takes a while for narcissists to take off the mask they wear most of the time and show their true face. Once they do, what is under that mask is abusive behavior.

This abusive behavior becomes psychological and verbal abuse and sometimes physical and sexual as well. Normally, the word abuse is associated with physical abuse or sexual abuse. In reality, the most common form of abuse among narcissists is psychological and/or emotional abuse.

That range of abusive behavior can vary from a subtle "well, and the truth is that that dress fitted you better five years ago" through "the truth is that sometimes you are a little childish" to a direct and extreme "you are crazy" or "you are bipolar."

- **There is no "we."**

Peg Streep answers in Psychology Today, the question "Can a narcissistic become more empathetic?" According to this professor of Philosophy and Gender,

Women and Sexuality Studies at the University Gustavus Adolphus in Minnesota, "Lack of empathy of the narcissist is the key to understand why, when you are with one, there is a perception that he/she is not there with you. "

Without empathy, a person remains as in a plastic capsule, without being able to be moved by the feelings or suffering of others. Empathy is a prerequisite (such as vulnerability and trust) in a relationship. Most studies focusing on the narcissism-relationship correlation have concluded that narcissists cannot have a healthy relationship because ultimately they turn out to be numb and lacking reciprocity.

- **It is (probably) impossible**

In the play "The Dream of a Summer Night," Shakespeare writes, "The becoming of true love never easily developed."

As far as a narcissist is concerned, the relationship will never have true love and will never develop easily. Each and every one of the demonstrations of affection is not an end in themselves but means to achieve an end. That end is what determines the narcissist. In this case, as we are talking about sentimental relationships, it is probably about love or sex, but they also tend to go after money, admiration, shelter, and attention among many more of their needs.

The victim may think that he is "in the future" of true love, but this is because he still does not see (or he does see it, but due to cognitive dissonance, he manages to justify it) the unbalanced demonstrations of manipulation, abuse, domination, and control by the narcissist.

If you are in a relationship with a person and you feel that some of what is told here applies, you better put some distance and perspective and determine if the relationship is actually healthy for you. The more time you spend in a relationship with a narcissist, the harder it is to end the relationship. These are the people who do not know how to let go, very tenacious, and who do not admit a "no" for an answer. So, you better think about letting go—sooner, the better!

CHAPTER 11

PEOPLE WHO DON'T CARE ABOUT YOU

Narcissistic friends are those who spend hours telling us about their problems and experiences without even being able to ask us how the day went. It's that person who is always late, who always does the most unlikely things when we need them. It's, in essence, a figure that we sooner or later wonder if it's worth keeping in our lives. Unreliability is the hallmark of a narcissistic personality.

Why do we get to establish a friendship with this type of profile? This is perhaps the first question that comes to mind. Now, a simple aspect should be noted. Too many (and most viewed the subject from the outside), it may seem simple that "if I have a narcissistic friend, I read him, and that's it."

However, things are not always so simple when we talk about human relationships. First is the bond of affection. Sometimes, we maintain for decades one more link by habit because there are many years and many shared experiences. Other times, we are not fully aware that this person responds to a narcissistic profile until the damage accumulates, until the erosion suffered by that bond is irreparable.

Narcissistic friends, how they behave, and why do they act this way?

For starters, narcissism falls within a spectrum. There are people with mild narcissistic traits and profiles that would already present a narcissistic personality disorder. Studies, such as that conducted by Dr. Elizabeth L. Kacel, from the University of Florida (United States), indicate that the origin of this behavior often depends on three dimensions: genetics, neurobiology, and environmental factors.

Thus, an aspect that usually explains a large part of these behaviors in narcissistic friends is the effect of an unfavorable family environment. They seek the validation they did not have in their childhood. They long for the recognition they did not have in the past, and often, they tend to repeat those abusive behaviors that their parents probably exercised with themselves.

Understanding this can explain many things to us. However, it is also essential to recognize what patterns and behaviors characterize narcissistic friends.

Monothematic conversations

The foothold on which the whole conversation revolves is themselves. It does not matter that the dialogue starts from something casual, from something that has happened to us or from the news of the present day. The narcissistic friend will always take him to his field. It's a unilateral talk revolving around him/herself.

Unplanned things always happen

If they are late, it is because they have had a mishap. If they have not been able to be with you when you needed them, it is because something unexpected and almost always serious happened to them, something that far exceeds what might happen to you. They are the people who are hard to trust because you know they will not be there, those who are always caught by the unexpected, the most unusual things we can imagine. With this, they always achieve what they most desire: to be the center of attention.

Minimize your problems and magnify theirs

It doesn't matter what happened to you at work, with your partner with your family. What you have in mind and that worries you will be insignificant when you explain it to a narcissistic friend. It will not only minimize what happened, but what will undervalue. What you can explain, he or she has also lived (and if he has not done so, he will invent it).

With this, it shifts the attention from you to him, to put the focus on himself. Boycotts you and with it manages to be once again the protagonist in the theater of life.

They won't be happy about your successes, and they won't share your happiness

Narcissistic friends generally have low self-esteem and low self-concept. Something like that implies something that can be very destructive in the long run: they will always prefer us at or below their height. That is, they will tune in more with us if we are unhappy, if our ability to achieve is minimal, if we are insecure, if we are permanent tenants in our comfort zone.

Now, when successes come, when we reach goals and feel happy, they will once again minimize every achievement. And they will do it for a very simple reason: they feel envious. They are unable to control that state, that harmful and dangerous emotion, with which they can harm us a lot if we do not put containment barriers. They cannot bear someone taking the lead.

What can we do with narcissistic friends?

Narcissistic friends are not good for travel companions in the adventure of life. They put us on brakes, blur the landscape, they don't let us see, and they even take us in the wrong ways. Therefore, we could say that the best thing will undoubtedly be to leave them at the nearest station and thus travel lighter, freer, and better health. Whatever you do for them, they will reciprocate with negativity.

However, as we have indicated at the beginning, narcissism enters into a continuum. There will be people, friends who deserve second chances. Hence, it is essential that they understand the effect (and consequences) of their acts and behaviors. Instead, there will be profiles that do not meet our suggestions and notices.

In those cases where the will to change is void, and where there is a clear refusal to seek expert help, the most reasonable thing is undoubtedly to take more drastic measures and in line with the most important thing: to maintain our own health and well-being.

CHAPTER 12

HOW TO DEFEND YOURSELF FROM PSYCHOLOGICAL ABUSE

More often than we would like, the world is not as lovely as it should be. It is not uncommon to come across indifference or lack of solidarity, but you learn to deal with them. The bad thing is that sometimes you not only have to face the coldness of the surroundings but almost imperceptibly end up feeling the victim of psychological abuse with all the letters.

It occurs in a supermarket when you are deliberately robbed of your place in line. It also happens at work if you are unlucky to fall for those bosses who are more dictators. Abuse also appears more and more often in schools and, why not, inside your own home.

It's everywhere

In front of the abusive subject, there are some who can react effectively. They put a limit on psychological aggression without much thought. On the contrary, others respond by being even more abusive, and the outcome is always unpredictable. The one who is best trained to psychologically abuse others wins, although they usually negotiate to get even.

But in many people, especially if they have received a very restrictive, overprotective education or have doubts about themselves, childhood fears, the fissures of self-image emerge. They are the favorite victims of abusers. They know that a frightened person is a breeding ground for their own petty empire of arbitrariness.

A very strong bond then forms: the abuser desperately needs his victim to compensate for his narcissistic need for power, and the victim feels that it is completely impossible to escape his attacker, who does not have the attributes necessary to do so. The victim finds himself in a definitely vicious trap.

The bad news is that breaking this infernal circle requires a large investment of energy and value. The good news is that even in the most extreme cases, it is possible to get out of there**. The question Is: how?**

Leaving the circle of psychological abuse

The first task is to recognize your victim status. Please do not fall into the temptation to justify the mistreatment you receive. Every abused person feels inward that he deserves it one way or another. This is a lie. It is an unconscious reaction that is due to conflicts with yourself and authority figures in your past.

Your next step should be to find support in others. Do not look for someone who will "save" you. Start simply by exposing your situation to people you trust. Whether solidarity is part of the problem (as often happens) does not matter. Look for a priest. Talk to the manicure. Tell a neighbor. The important thing here is not that you find guidance, but that you verbalize what has been going on. Doing so is very likely to make you feel stronger and stronger. Catharsis works wonders!

Identify the expressions the abuser uses to intimidate you. Analyze them. Remember that abuse is in every statement that questions your value or diminishes you as a human being. Faced with these statements, begin to oppose language formulas that reaffirm your presence. For example, in front of the classic "You Can't…", answer with "Maybe not right now. But I want to learn to be able, and I will try. "

Then you should gradually widen the emotional distance with the abuser. Never confide in him and start moving him away from the private aspects of your life. Don't negotiate, stand firm. When you feel it is the moment, start expressing your discomfort clearly and directly by the way he treats you. Do not accuse him. Doing so will give you a footing to make a long list of excuses. You better tell him what you feel: "When you scream, I feel scared, and I don't want to feel that way."

Extend the scope of these actions more and more, and you will see how, step by step, you will step out of the abusive circle. If the situation is more serious and involves psychological or physical danger to you, do not doubt it: you need to ask for professional help. It is your obligation to consult a psychologist and a lawyer. Do this as soon as possible, and do not allow yourself to postpone it.

CHAPTER 13

HOW TO DEFEND YOURSELF FROM EMOTIONAL TAKERS

Emotional takers are like black holes that swallow everything around them. They drain our energy with their demands, wear us out with their behavior, their complaints, manipulation, or personal injury. There are taking parents, partners, friends, and even children to whom we bestow the power of abuse and the loss of our authority and dignity.

Mark Twain said with a touch of irony that the principle of giving and receiving requires sufficient skill to give something and receive ten times more in return. Now, something that experts like Adam Grant, a professor at the University of Pennsylvania and author of the book *"Give and Receive"* explain to us, is that borrowers would not exist without the creditors. That is, sometimes, we fall into this spiral of unbalanced exchange: we allow the balance to always tilt to the same side.

Creditors have a distinct characteristic: They like to receive more than they give. They use reciprocity to their advantage, putting their own interests before the needs of others.

It is not a matter of looking for culprits. It is just to become aware that in all kinds of interaction, there is an exchange. We offer our time, give ideas, encouragement, and advice, and trust others and others trust us in return. However, there are those who have the inherent ability to emit light, to give that nurturing affection that always encourages and propels one to move on. They do this without realizing it because innate donors understand the life that way.

Undoubtedly, next to a giver, there will always be a taker. Someone who will be getting stronger, someone who (and don't forget that) always has a radar to identify more donors and feed on them without any embarrassment.

Are emotional takers born with this trait? OR Are they transformed?

Given this question, we can say that there are no conclusive studies to clarify this fact. However, a pediatrician and researcher William Sears, known for his work on parental attachment, introduced in the 1990s the term "high-demand babies." According to this expert, there are babies who come into the world with more intense emotional needs. These are the children with difficulty in falling asleep and whose education is usually much more complex and demanding.

This could be an explanation for the fact that there are people who are more likely to receive than to offer, better positioned to be served than to give attention. However, there are many subject matter experts who advocate another idea, another no less interesting and even revealing approach. Emotional takers are narcissistic personalities.

Emotional takers represent yet another face of **narcissism**. There is a sense of superiority in them that validates them to be the center of attention. To take control of every conversation, have exclusivity in any initiative, authority in any project, attention under any circumstances, and forgiveness in any wrongdoing. They are that black hole that sucks everything and steals all the energy, right, and self-esteem of the people around it.

Most of us are donors in our friendship and couple relationships. And as we are this way, we believe that others are, and so it is so difficult to recognize emotional takers. Meanwhile, they have radar to recognize the donor.

How can I defend myself against emotional takers?

As we have said, emotional takers are very adept at recognizing a giver. However, anyone who is used to giving anything for nothing, who understands a relationship as a sincere exchange of affection and attention, is not able to detect a narcissistic taker until grave harm is caused.

Let's look at what we must do to defend ourselves against this personality profile.

Listen to your body

Emotional takers cause discomfort. We may not be aware at first of their attitude, their tricks, and intentions. However, we will notice a contradiction within us, a feeling of physical exhaustion, fatigue when we spend time with this person.

Do not idealize or seek justification

When someone does something that bothers us, that causes us discomfort or generates contradiction, and we try to justify this behavior. We tell ourselves that the person may be stressed, did, or talked without thinking and will soon realize and ask for forgiveness. We idealize this person because he is our partner, our friend, our brother; we idealize because we love him, and without realizing it, we are feeding a taker.

We should be able to disable the filters we actually put in order to see others as they really are.

Remember what you deserve and let them know: Be Assertive

We might suggest here that the best strategy to defend ourselves against emotional takers would be to distance ourselves from them. However, this is not always possible and not even smart. The narcissistic taker must be aware of the effect of his actions and, for that, nothing better than to make him see what our limits are, what the consequences of their actions are (and maybe).

- Anyone who comes first under any circumstances and anytime sooner or later is no longer a priority.
- Those who believe they deserve more than others sooner or later will receive indifference.

We must practice zero tolerance on those who are used to crossing our limits. Therefore, always using assertiveness, we must demonstrate all that we do not tolerate, what we need, what we are willing to give, and what we expect to receive in return.

CHAPTER 14

TOXIC AND UNPRODUCTIVE ENVIRONMENTS

An organizational climate marked by tension, anxiety, criticism, and low productivity, narcissists at work undermine all dynamics, initiative, and even the simplest activities.

These are the profiles that must always be the center of attention and carry all merits through a strategy as elemental as destructive: sabotaging the rights and welfare of others.

Experts in personality psychology indicate that all of us, at some point in our lives, will encounter someone with a narcissistic profile. However, when we encounter a co-worker, manager, or any other position in a work context, the situation becomes complicated and exhausting.

Let's think our workdays cover a large part of our time. To this, we must add the financial factor, the productive factor, and the personal projection that we want to make in our career or within a company.

Thus, having a harmful and toxic presence can cause all these goals to be clearly wiped out.

"To join with mediocre people is to join with toxic people without realizing that addicted air enters your pores and makes you sick."

-Bernardo Stamateas-

Dealing with narcissists at work on a daily basis is not easy. Their behavior is often as irrational as it is exhausting, and if we do not have strategies to defend ourselves, our quality of life can be affected.

Narcissists at work, how to recognize them?

Narcissists at work have many names. They are the profiteers, the abusive, the selfish, the ones who don't know how to work in teams, the ones who make individual decisions without telling anyone. They are, in essence, the ones that create a suffocating and unproductive climate to the point of extinguishing our motivation, initiative, and desire to work every morning.

Also, another aspect must be understood. There are people who may have either a narcissistic trait. Others, however, fit into the small percentage of the population with a clear narcissistic personality disorder.

There is, therefore, a spectrum in which certain people highlight each feature, and others may become more flexible and even correct their behavior when given a warning.

But let's look at narcissists at work, these more classic profiles that wreak havoc among colleagues and the organization itself.

- They seek to be the center of attention.
- They want to take all the merits.
- They make use of lies to get what they want.
- They do not hesitate to highlight others and ridicule them.
- They will never admit that others have done something well.
- They sabotage the work of others.
- They do not take responsibility for their mistakes, and they can blame others for their failures and incompetence.
- We are facing a personality marked by envy.
- They often induce others to perform unethical behaviors.

How to survive before narcissists at work?

Narcissists at work can make us feel drained, exhausted, sinking our hopes for professional growth. The issue is even more complex when this profile defines our superior or that manager who is always above the rights of his workers.

Thus, and when these situations become extreme, it will always be advisable to seek employment advice from the company concerned.

On the other hand, it is also advisable to know very clearly about certain aspects. Very basic dimensions that can help us keep track of our motivation or goals.

- **Meet the narcissist, understand your weaknesses**

The first key is basic: avoid falling into the narcissistic game. So it is interesting to remember that what this profile craves the most are admiration and recognition. Your weak point is your self-esteem; let's never forget that.

A narcissist always demands immediate attention; he feeds on it. Make him realize that for you, his presence is secondary, and your priority is your obligations, your work, and your goals. If the narcissist is our superior, we will avoid first obeying or immediately responding to his demands (especially if they are not relevant and are merely seeking to highlight us).

- **Your needs are ahead**

The narcissist demands, humiliates, only thinks about himself, and sees no more ground than what surrounds his own person. In the face of this behavior, let us enforce our needs and our rights.

If something does not seem right to us, let us justify reason by speaking in the first person assertively to show their lack of empathy; We will not give in or fall into your suffocating network.

- **All in writing**

Narcissists at work, as we already know, do one thing: to demand from others. Therefore, it is best that all demands are in writing, in whatever form, by email, message, etc.

If at any time, contradictory information arises or an incident occurs, we need to be able to demonstrate where a particular order or requirement came from.

- **Don't fall for their traps**

The narcissist always longs to know things about us to use them to his advantage. In addition, it is common for him to seek our closeness at first to create complicity and information.

Let's avoid falling into his/her pitfalls, let's avoid talking about our personal lives, be cautious about sharing information and opinions with that kind of profile, because at any moment he/she can use them against us.

- **Clearly know your values and labor rights**

One of the most common problems associated with this personality is the lack of ethics. It sabotages the rights of others and, worse, can lead them into illegality.

Therefore, it is vital that we remember what our values are and are well informed about our labor rights. Narcissistic managers, for example, know how to manage their subordinates and employees to achieve their personal (not organizational) goals through illegal and unethical means.

So let's avoid regretting acts that we can prevent by being assertive and remembering where the limits are. Drawing the red line is crucial in the process.

CHAPTER 15

MANIPULATE OTHERS

The handlers are in almost all the places we visit in our daily lives. It could be your boss, your neighbor, a co-worker, a client, a distant relative, someone close, or any friend. We are talking about people who master certain techniques and use them to confuse us. However, can you identify the signs of psychological manipulation?

Although they are around us, it is not easy to detect these people. Their characteristics and personality traits are not evident. No one carries a sign in front of the warning that they are a narcissist or sociopath. So how can we avoid them?

Why did he choose me?

These types of people feed on the pain of others. So it is not because you are weaker, more vulnerable, or special, but simply another victim to them. It's an extra number. They are always bent upon preying anyone with the vulnerabilities.

When we are involved in certain situations, we all experience guilt or distrust. And the worst is that we blame ourselves without knowing how and why. But the fact is that the consequences disturb us, weaken our morale, complicate our lives, and increase our insecurities. How can they do this without our noticing?

What do handlers look for?

In fact, there are many types of manipulative people: sociopaths, narcissists, liars, or so-called emotional vampires. And detecting them is more a practical matter than a theoretical one. So if you were a victim at some point in your life, it would be easier for you to deal with such people the next time you encounter them.

However, we can say that the goals of manipulative people are very clear, instrumental, and they follow a certain pattern. Knowing what they are, it will be easier to notice the signs of psychological manipulation. Here are some of them:

- Override your will-power: Sow doubts so that you remain under your protection.
- Destroy your self-esteem: Devalue everything you do or have done. They do not take constructive criticism, only point out your shortcomings.

- Passive-aggressive revenge: They punish you with their contempt. When you need them, they put you aside; all you have to do is ask them something to disappear or even talk to you again.
- They misrepresent reality: They satisfy themselves by confusing people and creating discussions and misunderstandings. Once they have generated a discussion, they are left out having fun with each other's disputes.

Signs Of Psychological Manipulation Present In Each Technique.

The consequences of manipulation can create a very deep mark on each of us. Therefore, we need to know which manipulation techniques are most commonly used. The point is to learn to anticipate so that we are not puppets in the hands of others. It can help us be proactive, enabling us to prevent ourselves being the victims of the vicious game.

Many times, these people laugh at our opinions, blame us or make us feel guilty, subtly attack us, interrogate us, hide what doesn't interest them, lie, and so on. All to control the situation. But what manipulation techniques do they use?

The Gaslighting is a deliberate form of lying used to confuse the victim to get some benefit from him/her.

"It never happened," "Did you imagine," or "Are you crazy?" are some of the expressions used to distort and confuse your sense of reality by making you believe in something that didn't happen.

They give the victims a great sense of anguish and confusion to the point that they no longer trust themselves, their own memory, perception, or judgment.

- **Projection**

The handler transfers his negative characteristics or the responsibility for his behavior to the other person. The narcissists and psychopaths use it too, saying that the evil that surrounds them is not their fault, but the other person's.

- **Nonsense Conversations**

Ten minutes of talk is enough for you not to want to hear anything else. The handlers say nonsense, illogical explanations, and smoke screens, past events and so on.

They just try to entangle each other. They make monologues and try to engage you with their conversations. Advice? Runaway quickly! And if you can get out in 5 minutes, the better. Your mind will thank you.

- **Generalizations and disqualifications**

They make general, vague, and meaningless statements. They may seem intellectual, but in reality, they are people without content. Their conclusions are very general; your goal is to reject it and underestimate their opinions.

He tells you, for example, "you always want to be right," "everything bothers you," "you never agree on anything." "Keep Calm," "Thank You," or ignore a categorical "I think you're a little upset, we'll talk later."

- **Absurd situations**

Remember that the handler seeks to undermine your self-esteem and make you rethink everything you believe. They can put words in your mouth, things you didn't say. They will make you believe that they have the power to "read your mind." But no, it's just tricks and maneuvers. You can react with a mock submission: tell him he is right, but keep his position. You can also respond to your blackmail with an "ok" or laconic phrases.

The important thing is to take your self-esteem out of your hands. What they want is to throw it to the ground and then control it. Once they have weakened it, the task will be much easier for them.

- **Disguise of kindness**

"Yes, but..." If you just bought a house, they will tell you that it is a pity that you do not have another on the beach. If you look more elegant than ever, you will be told that other earrings would have gotten better on you. If you have completed a flawless report, you will be noticed that it is not stapled correctly.

But don't let it affect you; you know "your value"! Their achievements and virtues are worth much more than these signs of psychological manipulation. Don't give you credibility and stand by people who spend more time emphasizing what's right and encouraging you; those people who praise you when you deserve it and make constructive, non-destructive criticism.

- **Resist your temper tantrums**

When you oppose a manipulator, it is normal for his anger to increase within a few seconds, especially if you do not get into his game: your tolerance for frustration is usually not too high. He may begin to say atrocities and even insult you. It may refer to you in derogatory terms. It is the result of your own distrust.

CHAPTER 16

DEAL WITH TOXIC PEOPLE

Dealing with toxic people is a situation that, at some point in life, we will have to go through.

You may come across narcissists, liars, compulsives, manipulators, just to mention a few.

The problem with toxic people is that even if you want to avoid them, they always find a way to get into your life. Your actions are born of the need to belong to some group, and you can be the chosen one.

Luckily, there are some alternatives that smart people use to prevent toxic people from settling into their lives once they have been identified.

Let's look at a lot of advice for dealing with toxic people. Enjoy them! Smart people:

1. Do not pay attention to toxic people

What toxic people seek the most is attention. They want someone to see them and make them feel important. At any cost, they will endeavor to focus on each event or situation.

When you realize that one of these people has got

your wish, ignore him/her and pay no attention to him/her. If the toxic person dominated a conversation, change the subject, and give others the opportunity to talk.

Most often, this person will try to draw the conversation where he or she feels safe. You can avoid this by explaining that the topic is past and are now in another subject.

In a matter of minutes, the toxic person will walk away. Over time, such people will move away completely when they notice that they do not receive the attention they seek.

2. Don't tell your gossip secrets

How bad can a person who can't keep a secret do! Toxic people have no problem disclosing what you said. In addition, they criticize and talk badly behind your backs. Obviously, they are not the kind of people you can confide in.

Identifying these people is sometimes tricky because they often seem trustworthy and kind. But there are signs that will help you:

- They speak ill of others.
- Always comment on the secrets entrusted to them.

- They look for people to trust them as soon as they know them.
- When you make a comment about someone else, they will tell her/him.

The best antidote for gossip lovers is to tell them nothing. Simply live your life without inviting them. If they have entered your social circle, keep your distance.

3. Spend time, a lot of time, with your real friends

Smart people know that having a strong support network is important in life. When you have this, you don't even have to worry about toxic people. You will simply have people who support you the moment you need it.

Smart people know that true friends are more valuable than any material good.

4. Avoid Handlers

Smart people know that manipulators can ruin a life. People who manipulate hurt to reach their goals.

To avoid handlers, you first need to learn to identify them. You will know that they are manipulative because all their feelings become negative.

5. Let liars get involved in themselves

Toxic people often lie compulsively to other people and to themselves. They need to convince themselves that they are telling the truth to feel better. Unfortunately, for them, lies are always discovered.

Smart people don't get mad at lies, nor argue, just let the truth fall by its own weight. It does not take long for their falsehood to be exposed blatantly.

This usually happens sooner or later, because maintaining a false story is difficult, and contradictions do not take long to appear.

6. Do not engage in drama or discussion

Toxic people are experts at arguing for anything. If something doesn't go their way, get ready for a discussion and drama that will last for hours.

They like everyone to know about their problems. They love to be the center of attention and do not miss the opportunity.

If you are in this situation, act rationally. Try to talk to the toxic person calmly if you cannot finish the discussion by explaining that you will not be able to come up with a solution and ask for it later.

If the problem has no solution or the person does not want to solve it, simply say that it is no longer your business.

CHAPTER 17

SEXUAL NARCISSISM

Do you feel used by your partner or sexual partner? Does he or she only come to you when he/she wants sex? Does he/she care exclusively about his/her own pleasure, leaving aside your feelings? If you've been through this, pay attention to what we have to say about sexual narcissism.

Sexual narcissism shares many aspects of narcissistic personality disorder. In addition, it is specifically characterized by the following:

- Sexual self-centeredness (seek their own pleasure).
- Lack of empathy (They do not put themselves in the other person's shoes or care about their physical or emotional needs).
- Need for control and mastery over each other.
- They like relationships without commitment.
- Great sense of superiority.
- Excessive concern with the physical image

Sexual Narcissism

First, people with a high degree of sexual narcissism tend to be very competent in the art of seduction. Generally, they are endowed with good physical appearance, dialectical ability, and they are apparently attentive and caring towards others, especially those who do not know them very well.

Another feature of sexual narcissism is that, at first, the people who possess it can be very attractive. This way, your appearance, confidence in yourself, your determined actions can please the people around you, especially those with a more dependent profile or low self-esteem.

We now know that sexual narcissists appear to have a false sense of competence or personal worth. In fact, being so self-centered makes it impossible for them to focus on others. This way, they will never put themselves in the shoes of others; they can be very insensitive and lack empathy.

The other side of sexual narcissism

When someone falls into the clutches of the sexual narcissist, at first, there are only good times, laughter, and pleasure. However, over time, the victim finds that things are not going well. Suddenly, he discovers the other side of sexual narcissism.

Over time, this seducer will leave a growing void. With regard to sexual encounters, they only occur when that person wants, and in the way he/she wants. Also, they don't care about their partner's sexual needs. So what was once passion is now suffering? In short, sex becomes something humiliating.

In this case, you may disapprove of the attitude of the person with sexual narcissism, but he will never acknowledge his mistakes or his lack of empathy. On the contrary, he can defend himself with the phrases like these:

- The problem is that you are very picky.
- This has never happened to me before.
- My ex-girlfriends have always told me that I'm the best.
- You may have physical problems that prevent you from reaching orgasm.
- Etc.

Sex becomes a punishment

Sex is a dangerous element when it enters into the power relations of the couple. In this sense, people with sexual narcissism will use sex as a weapon. So if they want to punish their partner - for whatever reason - they can use sexuality to do so, and most of the times, they may go to any extent possible, sexually speaking.

Thus, access to sex is subjected to the conditions imposed by sexual narcissistic. Above all, he will avoid maintaining a strong bond to protect himself emotionally from possible abandonment. Increasingly, the axis of the relationship revolves around sexual relations. These relationships are generally not satisfactory.

Sexual differences

There are certain manifestations related to sexual narcissism that are different in men and women:

The narcissistic sexual woman usually requires her partner to admire her. She will find the partner more or less attractive depending on the admiration that arouses in the other. Also, they will be more likely to punish their partner by leaving him or her without sex. Access to sex will be dependent on the degree to which the partner submits to their demands.

The man with sexual narcissism is usually indifferent to his partner's sexual satisfaction. He may be more likely to take advantage of his partner physically.

CHAPTER 18

EMOTIONAL ABUSE IN RELATIONSHIPS

Emotional abuse has many definitions but is best characterized by typical behavior patterns and relationship dynamics. Emotional abuse is primarily based on a power imbalance, where at least one person in the relationship tries to exercise psychological and sometimes physical control over the other. But emotional abuse does not involve physical aggression, per se. Interestingly, this type of abuse is not always conscious, obvious, or intentional, although at times, it is.

Someone who grew up in an emotionally abusive environment may not recognize their own abusive behavior. Or you may not recognize the abuse you suffered as such. One can also confuse control with caution, and see their dominating or invasive attitude, not only as appropriate and necessary but also as a sign of affection. It amounts to sheer mutilated interpretation of the situation.

Emotional abuse in marriage and relationships, in general, can be characterized in two ways. The most aggressive form of emotional abuse is evident and leaves the victim with a clear understanding of the experience. You know what the abuser feels and says about you as well as the other people in your life.

The most passive form is less characterized by domination but by annoying pinpricks. Small and seemingly insignificant implications or corrections that accumulate in a kind of master and subordinate relationship over time. And you can never really know what the abuser thinks, feels or says about you - or even how much abuse has affected you.

So how do you know if your spouse, partner, or someone in your life is emotionally abusive?

More Aggressive Signs Of Emotional Abuse

Swearing

They may use curses during an argument to scold the other, or in the day to day affairs, being childish and disrespectful. You are not stupid, useless, ugly, or any other degrading name.

Contempt and condescension

You are always below him. He needs to make you and your accomplishments seem useless and insignificant. And he can cause embarrassment in front of people who respect and care about you.

Condemnation and criticism

You can't do anything right. You are always wrong, no matter what. You are a bad person, a bad father, a bad friend, a bad follower. Or whatever else you can think of. Or at least you're not as good, or as skilled as he/she is.

Control and possessiveness

He tries to control his day, his location, his appearance, or priorities. You cannot go anywhere without him, without his permission, or without informing him first. If you do this, there will be a long talk or intense fight afterward.

Accusations and paranoia

Accusations of infidelity are the most typical. But the charges can be as strange as cheating on a friend, a family member, or for money. They may accuse you of stealing from them or even try to harm you or your children.

Threats

They could threaten violence, humiliation, or abandonment, which silences any objections to the torturous treatment.

Handling and corruption

She will want to keep an agenda that only benefits or appeals to her. Or that is harmful or offensive to you. She often convinces you to keep your commitments or tries to make you believe the idea came from you when it really wasn't.

Corruption and extortion

He will use a secret as an object of abuse, as a means to maintain and increase control.

Isolation

He prevents your contact with friends, family, co-workers, and others who care about your health and well-being, and generally with anyone else in the world. This helps keep your track. He wants you to be entirely dependent on him.

Exposure and voyeurism

He speaks ostensibly about abuse, freely and independently, and even about his achievements, in front of you and others. He can see you suffer for his control and humiliation, and invite other people to join him. He can even film as you scrub the floor, down and on your knees.

More Passive Signs Of Emotional Abuse

Guilt and shame

She tries to make you feel bad for something that is out of your control. When things go wrong, and they always go wrong in their presence, it's your fault. And even if you try your best to keep things organized, or fix them, your effort is still not enough.

Fault

The problem is always with you, and he does nothing wrong. You deserve the way he and others treat you. Again, you are responsible for what others do.

Comparison and disapproval

You're not good enough the way you are. You need to change. Or you need to be more like someone else. And yet, it probably still won't be good enough.

Correction

Mistakes are prohibited. She makes the rules and decides when and how to break them. Justified or not, she will find something you did wrong and let you know that. The sole motive is to undermine your self-esteem, obviously.

Gossip

He talks negatively or pitying you behind your back. Especially for other people who respect you to degrade their opinion of you, or for people who already see you negatively by adding firewood to the fire.

How to recover from emotional abuse

Recovering from emotional abuse first requires processing a traumatic experience that has undermined our self-esteem. To do so, it is necessary to avoid blaming yourself, because the mistake is never that of the one who trusts, who gives everything for a relationship. The "crime" is who lies, the narcissistic and insane person who does everything through manipulation, blackmail, and psychological abuse.

If we emphasize the importance of not taking full responsibility or blame for what happened, it is because it is a very concrete fact. When a person is finally able to leave an abusive relationship, it is very common for them or a member of their environment to think, "Why haven't you left that person before? How could you be so blind and not see everything that was going on? "

"The way is to calm the mind and make it look at itself realistically. A mature, balanced mind that knows how to lose. A humble mind, but not stupid. An open mind to the world, vigorous and down to earth. "

-Walter laugh-

Emotional abuse is not easy to unmask because its mechanisms are often very subtle, and at the same time, sophisticated. We must add yet another ingredient-- love. Because we must not forget that those who love are stubborn; they trust and commit. That is why these mechanisms are not visible to the naked eye, and if they are perceived, the brain applies very complex strategies to dissuade doubts, to clear a dense fog that prevents the person from seeing clearly what is happening.

Recovery From Emotional Abuse: A Battle Not Everyone Can Win

The cycle of emotional abuse often works as an addiction. There is a punishment-reward system in which we are stuck. In a moment, they give us unreasonable attention, the most incredible caresses, they are devoted and passionate, then comes the turn of the demands, the coldness, the humiliation, and the censorship that leaves sequels.

Affection is related to abuse in an infinite chain where we install ourselves as another piece of this machine controlled by the aggressor. Abandoning this dynamic is not easy at all. Also, let's not believe that by ending this relationship, we end the suffering.

Many people, men, and women, who finally manage to break out of an abusive relationship, innocently think that with this brave step, it is all over. They think that after this decision, everything will be better, that after reaching rock bottom, everything will suddenly improve and recovery will be immediate. However, it is not so.

Symptoms that you have not gotten over an abusive relationship

- Guilt. We direct ourselves a little anger that we didn't notice before and wasted so much time with someone who kept on hurting us.
- Guilt is accompanied by anger. We accumulate so much frustration and anger that we sometimes project this feeling on others at times.
- We become suspicious.
- We may go through periods of great hyperactivity, we want to do many things, get involved in different projects, but soon we feel exhausted, without energy.
- Our self-image, our perception of ourselves, and our self-esteem are still damaged, deeply wounded.
- We no longer have positive emotions of the same intensity as before, now joy is less great, illusion less motivating, dreams less hopeful. It's like we're anesthetized.

Key to recovering from emotional abuse

As we said earlier, recovering from emotional abuse requires reinterpreting our victim status so that it does not occupy our whole concept of ourselves, let alone guilt and defenseless behavior. In the long run, it can make the traumatic state chronic. The identity of the victim takes away our power and weakens our understanding of ourselves.

- **Focus: You are brave and must assume ownership of your own life**

You are not a victim; you are a brave person who must recover from a traumatic past. To do this, you must focus on the present moment and take the reins of your life. You are responsible for your own life, and responsibility means that you are "the one who knows how to respond to situations," so forget about guilt and be the owner of your reality. Memorize the "lesson" and move on with strength.

- **Faced with existential anguish, be calm**

Recovering from emotional abuse implies, as we said, learning to be responsible for ourselves in this new stage of our lives. In taking this step, it is common to feel anguish, fear, perplexity. When you have these feelings, the answer is "calm."

Take it easy, understand that no one will rush you to recover, understand and assume that every cure takes time, so there is no choice but to go at your own pace, listen to yourself and accept all your emotions. Little by little, you will control everything around you. Eventually, you will be able to assume full control of your own life.

- **Positive reality management**

After an abusive relationship, it is common to accumulate anger, to feel distrust, to have a negative image of ourselves because we feel victims of something we should have stopped as soon as possible. To avoid these feelings, we must apply a more positive approach to our surroundings.

If you feel angry, channel it, release it.

If you feel alone, talk to other people, support groups that have gone through the same as you.

If you find that you are not progressing, that all attempts return to this starting point where there are helplessness and frustration, seek professional help.

To recover from emotional abuse, you need to make a positive control of reality. We must apply a constructive approach where there is no shortage of resources, support, openness to the external environment, providing us with appropriate therapies and points of view that allow us to return to a lighter and brighter self. All the factors that help us regain the vitality of our psyche and personality, so that we are in charge of our own life again.

CHAPTER 19

HOW TO REBUILD MY SELF-ESTEEM AFTER THE RELATIONSHIP WITH A NARCISSIST

When it comes to repairing self-esteem after the relationship with a narcissist, what we need is self-care and courage. Combine courage to heal wounds and regain the lost confidence.

How to rebuild my self-esteem after the relationship with a narcissist? This is a question that many people often ask themselves. They do this by being aware of the consequences that remain after a bond based on suffering and constant manipulation. Thus, something that should be known in the first place is that this craftsmanship of reconstruction and healing is not an easy process.

There are those who have spent years with a narcissist. Life next to this personality profile implies, for example, that at any given time, the person opens their eyes, identifying several ideas that they had ignored. The first is that living with these people hurts. The second, there is usually a very long period when you are fully aware that the best thing is to end that relationship. However, the heart cannot; dependence is a very powerful glue fueled by fear.

There are many people who fear to end that link because they don't know how the narcissist will react. Moreover, something common is to fall into the rebound effect; that is, break the relationship and soon start it again. It is a way back and forth, where even though they make us promises that certain attitudes and behaviors will not be repeated, they are repeated and with the same impunity.

Leaving a narcissist is an act of need, courage, and health. The longer you will take, the worse will be the consequences. However, after the breakup, an important stage begins, the reconstruction of long-abused self-esteem.

"A selfish person is one who insists on talking about himself when you are dying to tell him about yourself."

-Jean Cocteau-

Keys to rebuild my self-esteem after the relationship with a narcissist

Broken bones heal. Wounds, burns, and chafing heal with proper care in a few weeks. However, injuries to the tissue of self-esteem, of self-concept, of one's own values and even of identity, do not heal with Betadine, or with antibiotics, or with the passage of time.

To rebuild your self-esteem after the relationship with a narcissist, you need concrete actions. It is not enough to let time pass because otherwise, the emptiness will remain there, and you will be basically the figures that walk the broken world. No one can find happiness again without the muscle of self-esteem recovered, because that psychological competence threads absolutely everything.

So let's see what approaches can help us rebuild it.

1. Blame it off, and it's time to rewrite

When we leave the relationship with a narcissist, many biases, words, and ideas remain in our minds to deactivate. Something that carries out this type of profile with its effective partners is reprogramming and cancellation. They make their victims believe that they are inferior, that they are not valid for what they want and that their needs are secondary. Therefore, we need to turn off certain images of our mind in order to overhaul the shattered psyche and self-esteem:

- You are not to blame for anything that happened. Whoever harms is the only culprit. However, it is worth nothing to focus on hate and resentment, either. You have to turn the

page, and more importantly, you must take control of your life.
- Make a list of those phrases and images that remain embedded in your mind (contempt, humiliation, situations in which you were always in the background, etc.).
- Assume that those memories cannot be erased, but the idea is that every day, they lose their power over you. Do not tear pages from the book of our life; just pass them and rewrite new chapters after learning from the experience.

2. **Empower yourself: I am, I am worthy, I can decide about my life**

At the end of the relationship with a narcissist, there is usually a whole cluster of insecurities. What do I do now? How do I take control of my life? How do I leave behind all the harmful memories? The key is to empower oneself and to empower ourselves; we must live in the present and not in the past.

- To achieve this, there is nothing better than starting new projects. Often, by feeling competent in new tasks, new jobs, and situations, the self-esteem regains its power. We give way to a new version of ourselves.

- Therefore, do not hesitate to meet new people, to make your days have new incentives to put you to the test: other jobs, courses, hobbies.

CONCLUSION

What a person with a narcissistic attitude needs is to train humility. Sometimes, small daily activities help, such as tolerating a long line or letting another one through first. It is also important to help you understand the importance of delegating and recognizing the positive acts of others.

These types of people need to be helped to understand the real scope of their own achievements and virtues. Using patience and respect, you can contribute to that person being loved more. To understand that he has real achievements, but these do not make him superior to others. He also has errors and failures, but these do not make anyone inferior.

The most important thing is that you do not fall into the trap of trying to "lower your fumes." This only leads you to create an enmity that prevents any progress. If something is lacking, the narcissist's real affection and real acceptance. Remember that love can do everything and more in cases where your absence becomes ill.

www.ingramcontent.com/pod-product-compliance
Lightning Source LLC
Chambersburg PA
CBHW070903080526
44589CB00013B/1169